Contents

D0472509

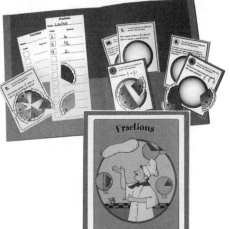

Math Centers
Take It to Your Seat

What's Great About This Book

Centers are a wonderful, fun way for students to practice important skills, but they can take up a lot of classroom space. The 15 centers in this book are self-contained and portable. Students may work at a desk or even on the floor using a lapboard for writing. Once you've made the centers, they're ready to use at any time.

Three Kinds of Centers

- Hanger Pocket Centers
- Shoebox Centers
- Folder Centers

Everything You Need

- Teacher direction page
  - How to make the center
  - Description of student task
- Full-color patterns needed to construct the center
- Reproducible answer forms

Using the Centers

The centers are intended for skill practice, not to introduce skills. It is important to model the use of each center before students do the task independently.

Considering these questions in advance will avoid later confusion:

- Will students select a center or will you assign them?
- Will there be a specific block of time for centers or will the centers be used throughout the day?
- Where will you place the centers for easy access by students?
- What procedure will students use when they need help with the center tasks?
- Where will students put completed work?
- How will you track the tasks and centers completed by each student?

Hanger Pocket Centers

Hanger pocket centers can be easily stored on a hook or rod anywhere in the classroom. Students hang the center on the edge of a desk or back of a chair while working on the task.

Basic Hanger Pocket Pattern

Materials

- hanger
- 17" x 36" (43 x 91 cm) piece of paper (large brown paper bag, butcher paper, shelf paper) or fabric

Steps to Follow

Butcher paper, shelf paper, fabric

Staple.

Fold twice.

Staple.

Brown Paper Bag

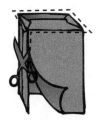

Cut up one side.
Cut out the bottom of the bag.

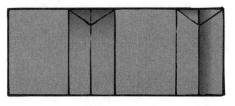

Open flat.
Attach to hanger as shown above.

Skip Counting

Cut water ripples out of a contrasting shade of blue.

Count by 2s.

Cut out the fish on page 5. Glue them to the top of the pocket.

Count by 5s.

Add kelp made from strips of green construction paper.

Count by 10s.

I can count by 10s.

Skip Counting

I can count by 2s.

Skip Counting

Cut a wavy line at the top of the pocket. Glue a contrasting shade of blue cut in a wavy line just inside the top of the pocket. Cut out the sign on page 7. Glue it to the pocket flap as shown.

Skip Counting

Preparing the Center

1. Using a 17" x 36" (43 x 91 cm) piece of blue butcher paper, prepare the top of the basic hanger pocket following the directions on page 3. Then follow the directions above to add details to the hanger pocket.

2. Laminate and cut apart the task cards on pages 9, 11, 13, and 15. Place each set of cards in its own envelope. Laminate and cut out the labels on page 7. Glue the labels to the appropriate envelopes. Place the envelopes of cards in the hanger pocket.

3. Place a supply of the answer forms on page 17 in the pocket.

Using the Center

1. The student takes a set of cards out of the fish hanger pocket and reads them. The student then puts the cards in order.

2. The student writes the task on the answer form, and then copies the numbers in order.

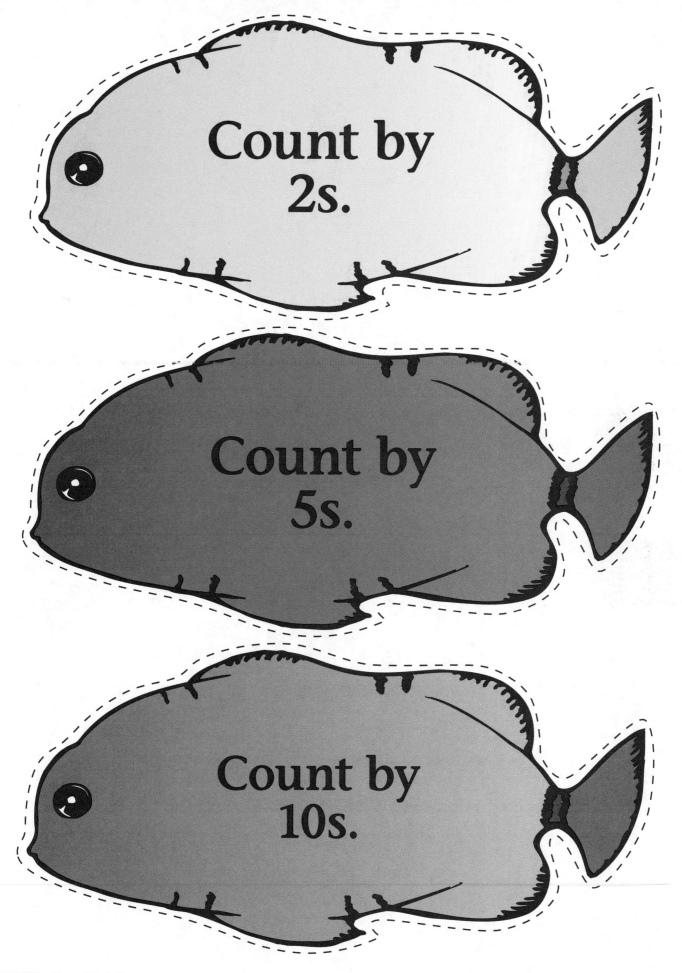

Count by
2s.

Count by
5s.

Count by
10s.

I can count
by 2s.

I can count
by 5s.

I can count
by 10s.

Skip
Counting

Math Centers - Take It to Your Seat • EMC 3013

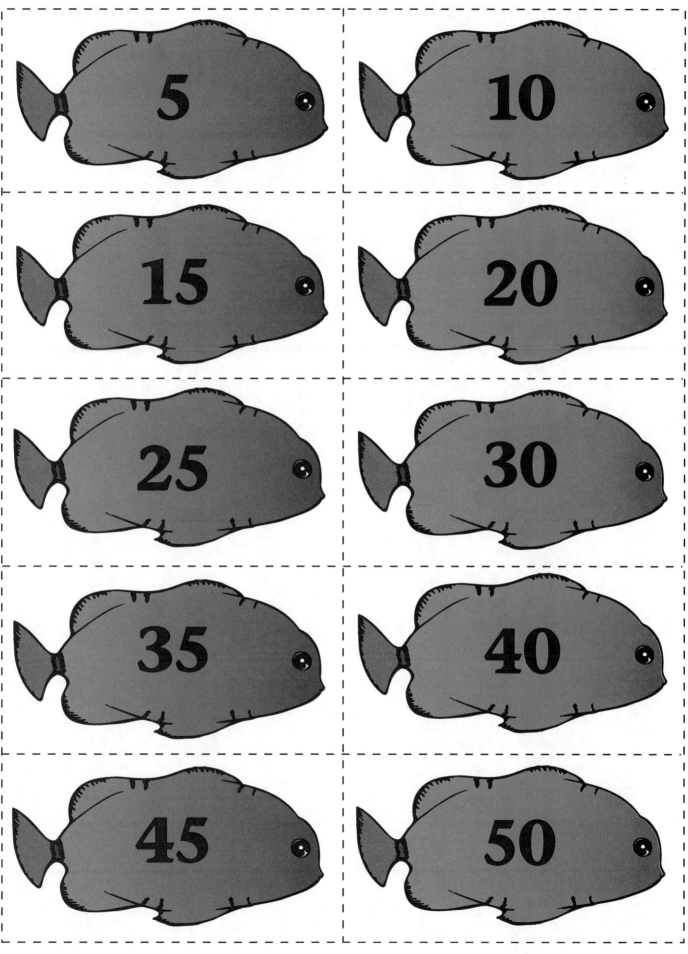

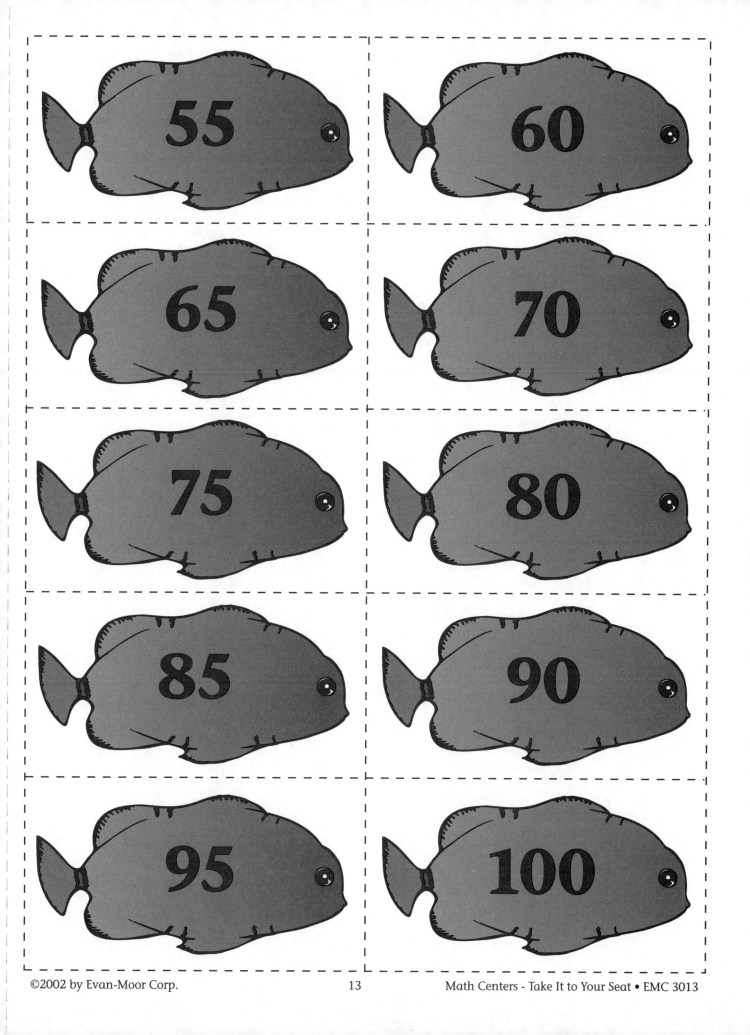

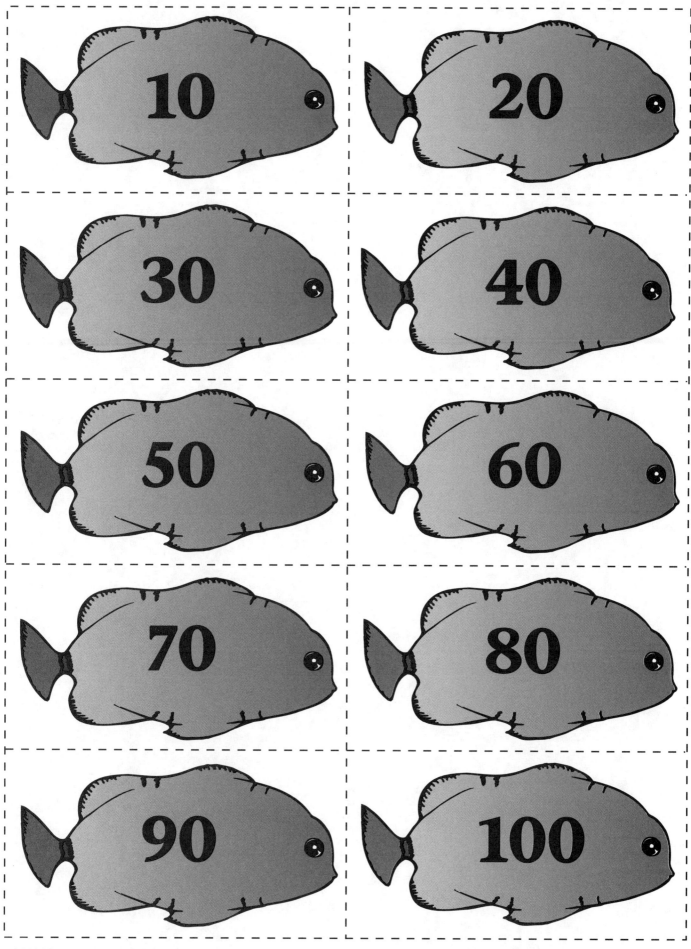

Skip Counting

Name _____

I counted by 2s   5s   10s

Write the numbers below.

_____ _____ _____ _____

_____ _____ _____ _____

_____ _____ _____ _____

_____ _____ _____ _____

_____ _____ _____ _____

Skip Counting

Name _____

I counted by 2s   5s   10s

Write the numbers below.

_____ _____ _____ _____

_____ _____ _____ _____

_____ _____ _____ _____

_____ _____ _____ _____

_____ _____ _____ _____

Skip Counting

Name _____

I counted by 2s   5s   10s

Write the numbers below.

_____ _____ _____ _____

_____ _____ _____ _____

_____ _____ _____ _____

_____ _____ _____ _____

Skip Counting

Name _____

I counted by 2s   5s   10s

Write the numbers below.

_____ _____ _____ _____

_____ _____ _____ _____

_____ _____ _____ _____

_____ _____ _____ _____

Counting Puzzles

Draw a mouth line and nostrils with a black marking pen.

Roll up a scrap of pink paper for the tongue. Glue it to the pocket.

Add eyes cut from two 3 1/2" x 5" (9 x 13 cm) pieces of green paper and two 2 1/2" x 4" (6.5 x 10 cm) pieces of white paper. Add round pupils cut from black scraps.

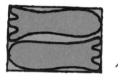

Add arms cut from a 6" x 9" (15 x 23 cm) piece of green paper. Attach them to the pocket with paper fasteners.

Use a contrasting shade of green for spots on the frog's body.

Counting Puzzles

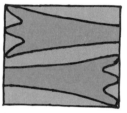

Add legs cut from a 10" x 12" (25.5 x 30.5 cm) piece of green paper.

Preparing the Center

1. Using a 17" x 36" (43 x 91 cm) piece of green butcher paper, prepare the top of the basic hanger pocket following the directions on page 3. Then follow the directions above to add details to the hanger pocket.

2. Laminate and cut out page 20. Glue the counting sign to the frog's pocket. Tape or glue the appropriate label to each envelope. Laminate and cut apart the puzzle pieces on pages 21 and 23. Place each set of pieces in the appropriate envelope. Place the envelopes in the frog's pocket.

3. Place a supply of the answer forms on page 19 in the pocket.

Using the Center

1. The student takes a puzzle out of the frog hanger pocket and puts it together.

2. The student then copies the numbers in order on the answer form, using as many lines as necessary.

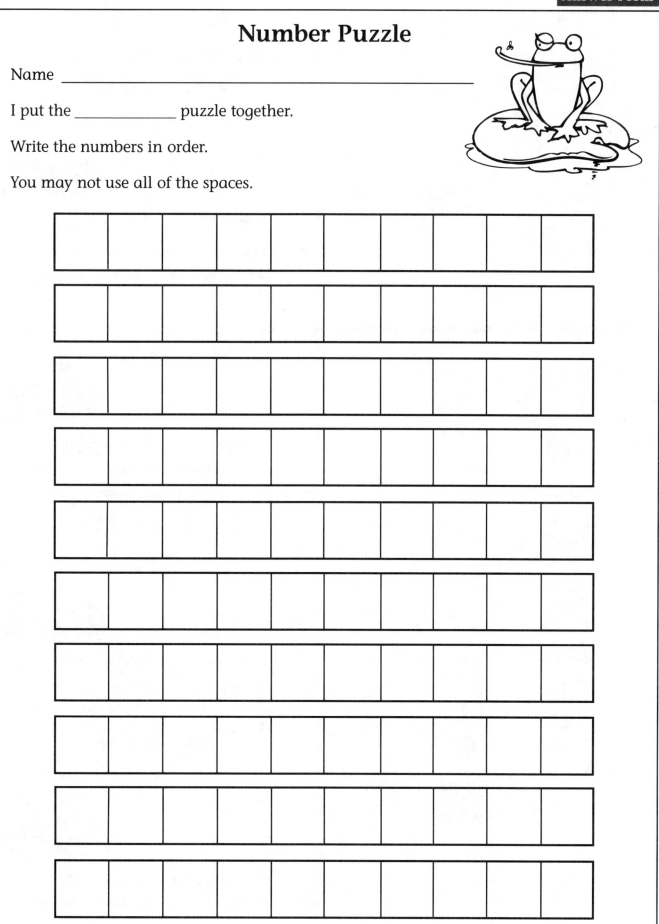

Number Puzzle

Name _____

I put the _____ puzzle together.

Write the numbers in order.

You may not use all of the spaces.

Counting Puzzles

Counting

I can count to 30.

Counting Puzzle

I can count to 40.

Counting Puzzle

I can count to 50.

Counting Puzzle

I can count to 100.

Counting Puzzle

1	2	3	4	5	6	7	8	9	10
11	12	13	14	15	16	17	18	19	20
21	22	23	24	25	26	27	28	29	30
31	32	33	34	35	36	37	38	39	40

1	2	3	4	5	6	7	8	9	10
11	12	13	14	15	16	17	18	19	20
21	22	23	24	25	26	27	28	29	30
31	32	33	34	35	36	37	38	39	40
41	42	43	44	45	46	47	48	49	50

1	2	3	4	5	6	7	8	9	10
11	12	13	14	15	16	17	18	19	20
21	22	23	24	25	26	27	28	29	30

1	2	3	4	5	6	7	8	9	10
11	12	13	14	15	16	17	18	19	20
21	22	23	24	25	26	27	28	29	30
31	32	33	34	35	36	37	38	39	40
41	42	43	44	45	46	47	48	49	50
51	52	53	54	55	56	57	58	59	60
61	62	63	64	65	66	67	68	69	70
71	72	73	74	75	76	77	78	79	80
81	82	83	84	85	86	87	88	89	90
91	92	93	94	95	96	97	98	99	100

Computation

Glue on large wiggle eyes.

Fold a 2 1/2" x 6" (6.5 x 15 cm) piece of orange construction paper in half. Cut the beak as shown.

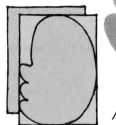

Using two 9" x 12" (23 x 30.5 cm) pieces of yellow construction paper, cut wings and attach them to the body with paper fasteners.

Cut a comb from a 4" (10 cm) square of red construction paper.

Cut a wattle from a 3" x 4" (7.5 x 10 cm) piece of red construction paper.

Preparing the Center

1. Using a 17" x 36" (43 x 91 cm) piece of yellow butcher paper, prepare the top of the basic hanger pocket following the directions on page 3. Then follow the directions above to add details to the hanger pocket.

2. Cut a nest from a 6" x 17" (15 x 43 cm) piece of brown construction paper. Laminate the nest and the computation sign and eggs on page 27. Glue the sign and eggs to the nest. Tape or glue the nest to the pocket flap as shown.

3. Laminate and cut out the work boards on pages 31, 32, and 33. Place these in the hen's pocket.

4. Laminate and cut out the number cards on page 29. Place them in an envelope or self-closing plastic bag and put it in the pocket.

5. Place a supply of the answer forms on page 26 in the pocket.

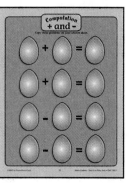

Using the Center

1. The student takes one work board and the number cards out of the hen hanger pocket.

2. The student creates addition, subtraction, or multiplication problems and their answers on the work board. He or she then copies the problems on the answer form.

Computation

Name _____

Copy your problems here.

Computation

Name _____

Copy your problems here.

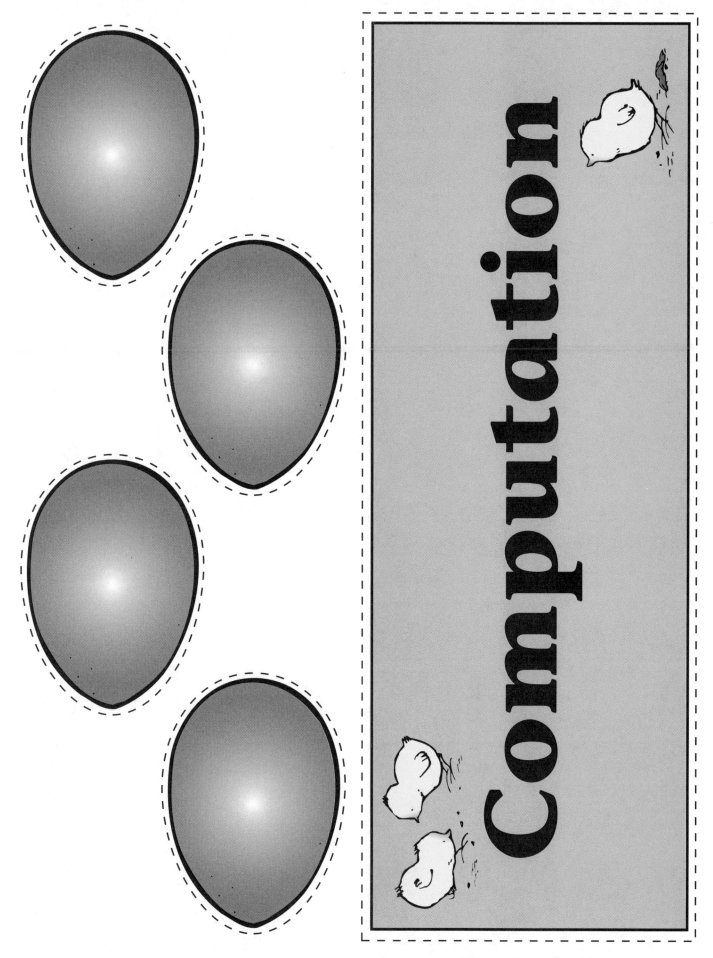

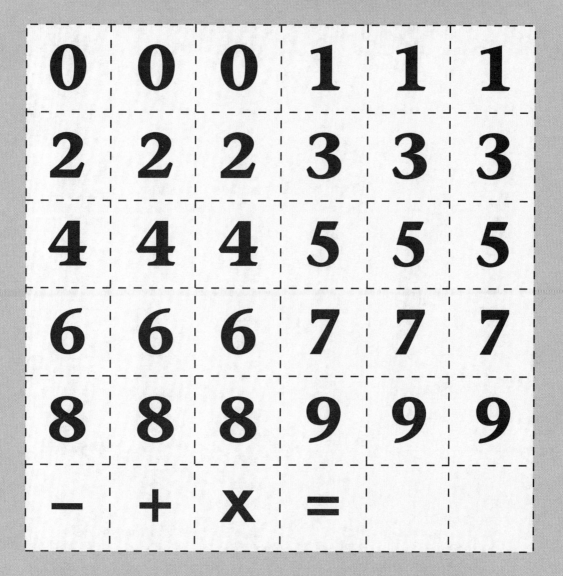

Glue this to the envelope.

Computation Number Cards

Computation
+ and -

Copy these problems on your answer sheet.

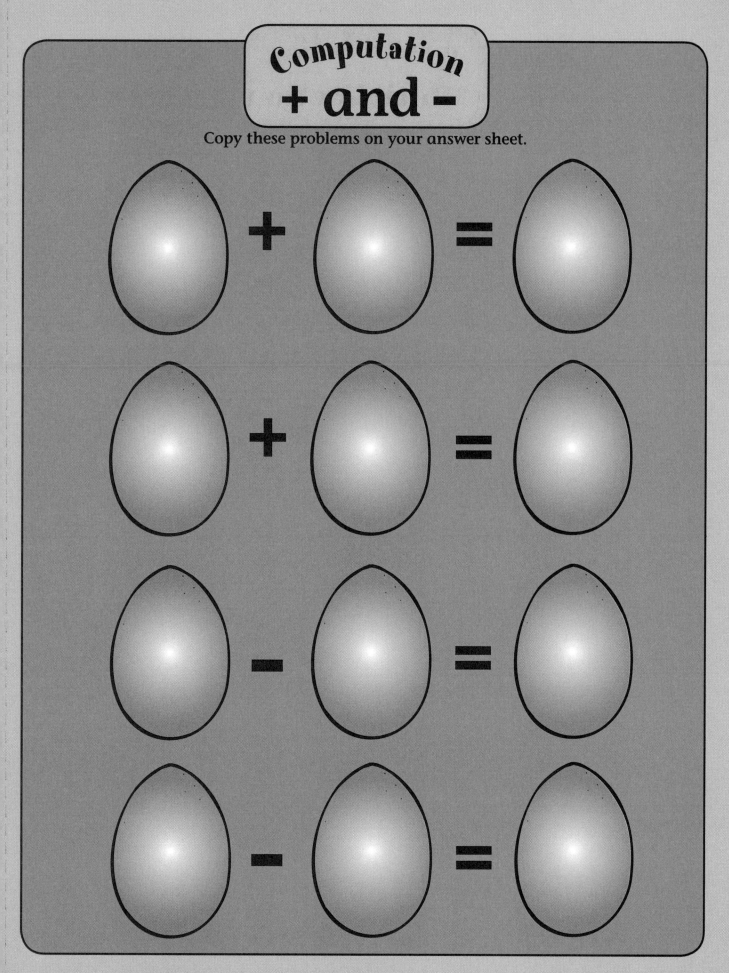

Computation
Multiplication

Copy these problems on your answer sheet.

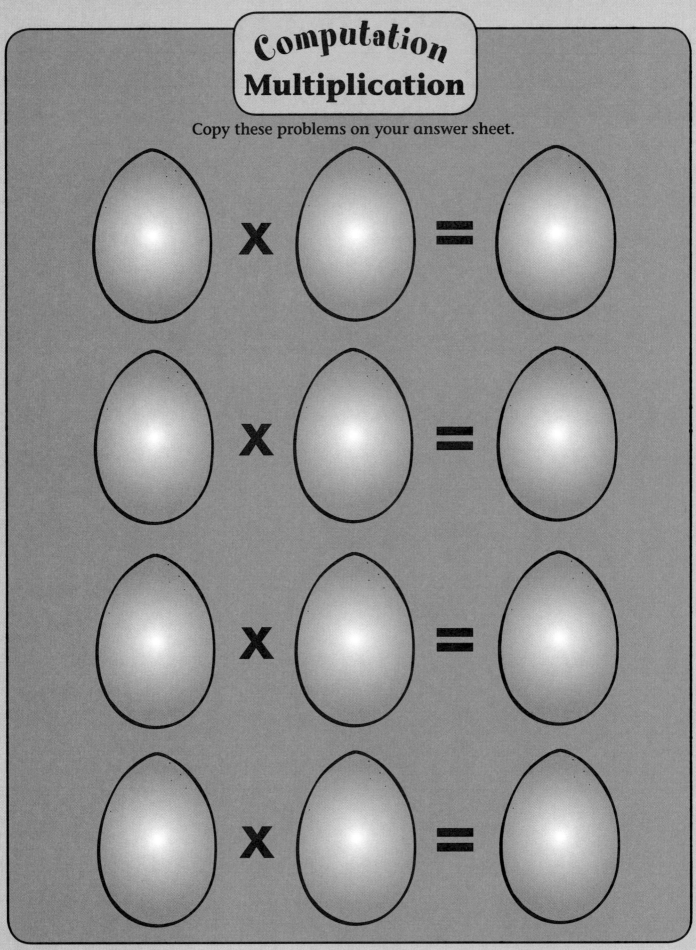

Copy the problem on your answer sheet.

Put a +,
−, or ✗ here.

Number Families

Use two 3 1/2" x 5" (9 x 13 cm) pieces of white construction paper for windows. Add details with marking pens and scraps of colored paper.

Using a 6" x 17" (15 x 43 cm) piece of red construction paper, cut a roof. Glue it to the house pocket. Cut a chimney from a 3" x 5" (7.5 x 13 cm) piece of black construction paper. Add a puff of smoke cut from a scrap of white paper.

Add a strip of green grass cut from construction paper along the top of the pocket flap.

Make a door from a 3 1/2" x 6" (9 x 15 cm) piece of red construction paper. Add details with marking pens and scraps of colored paper.

Preparing the Center

1. Using a 17" x 36" (43 x 91 cm) piece of light blue butcher paper, prepare the top of the basic hanger pocket following the directions on page 3. Then follow the directions above to add details to the hanger pocket.

2. Laminate and cut out the sign on page 37. Glue it to the house pocket flap.

3. Laminate and cut out the cards on pages 39, 41, 43, 45, 47, and 49. Place each color of computation card in a separate self-closing plastic bag.

4. Using the Number Family labels from pages 39, 41, 43, 45, 47, and 49, prepare the envelopes as shown.

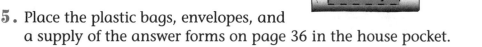

5. Place the plastic bags, envelopes, and a supply of the answer forms on page 36 in the house pocket.

Using the Center

1. The student takes one bag of cards and the three envelopes in the same color out of the pocket.

2. The student then "delivers the mail" to the correct envelope to build number families.

3. The student writes the number facts for each family on the answer form.

Number Families

Name _____

The _____ Family	The _____ Family	The _____ Family
_____	_____	_____
_____	_____	_____
_____	_____	_____
_____	_____	_____
_____	_____	_____
_____	_____	_____
_____	_____	_____

Can you
deliver
the mail?

MAIL

Number Families

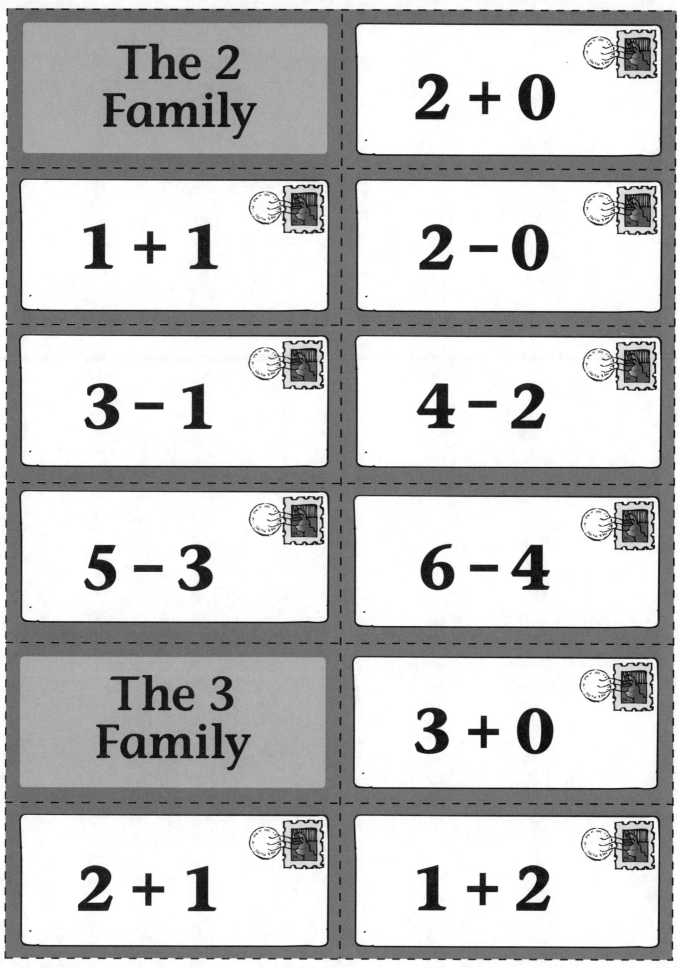

The 2 Family

2 + 0

1 + 1

2 - 0

3 - 1

4 - 2

5 - 3

6 - 4

The 3 Family

3 + 0

2 + 1

1 + 2

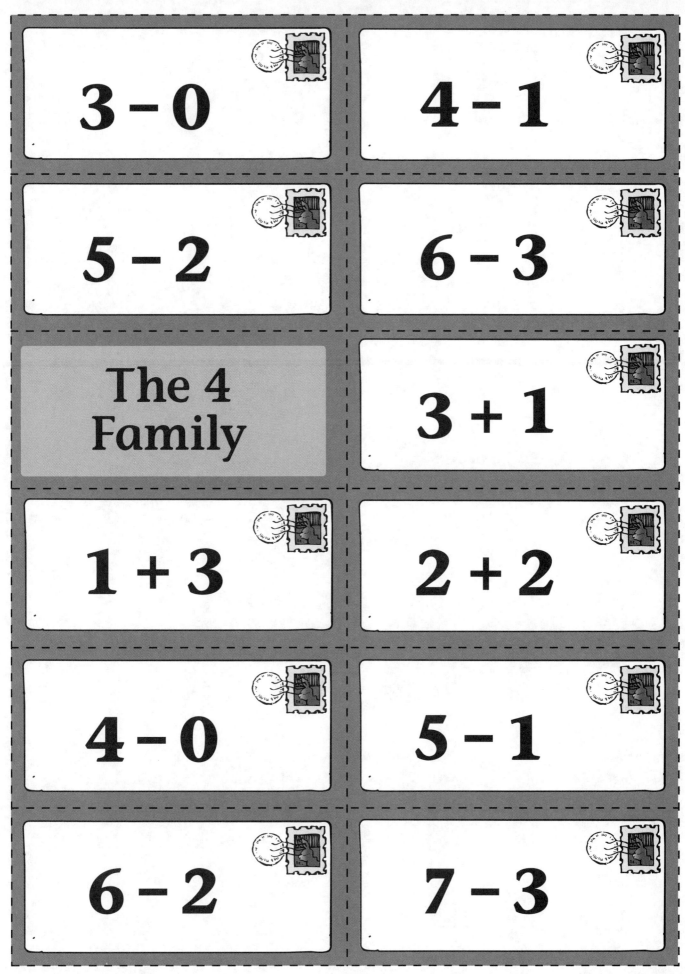

3 - 0

4 - 1

5 - 2

6 - 3

The 4 Family

3 + 1

1 + 3

2 + 2

4 - 0

5 - 1

6 - 2

7 - 3

Math Centers - Take It to Your Seat • EMC 3013

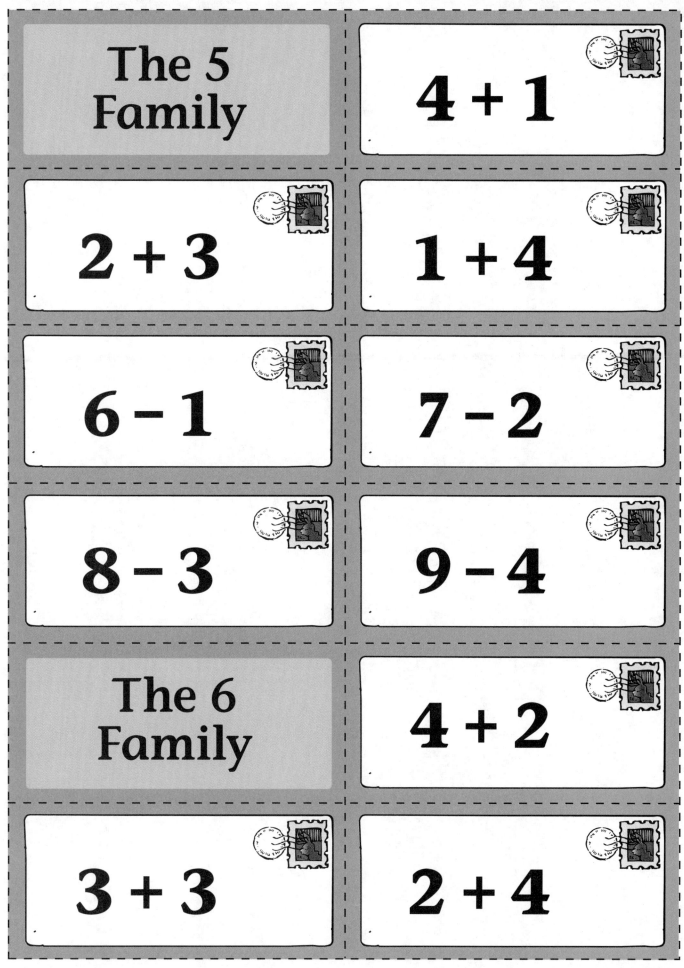

The 5 Family

4 + 1

2 + 3

1 + 4

6 − 1

7 − 2

8 − 3

9 − 4

The 6 Family

4 + 2

3 + 3

2 + 4

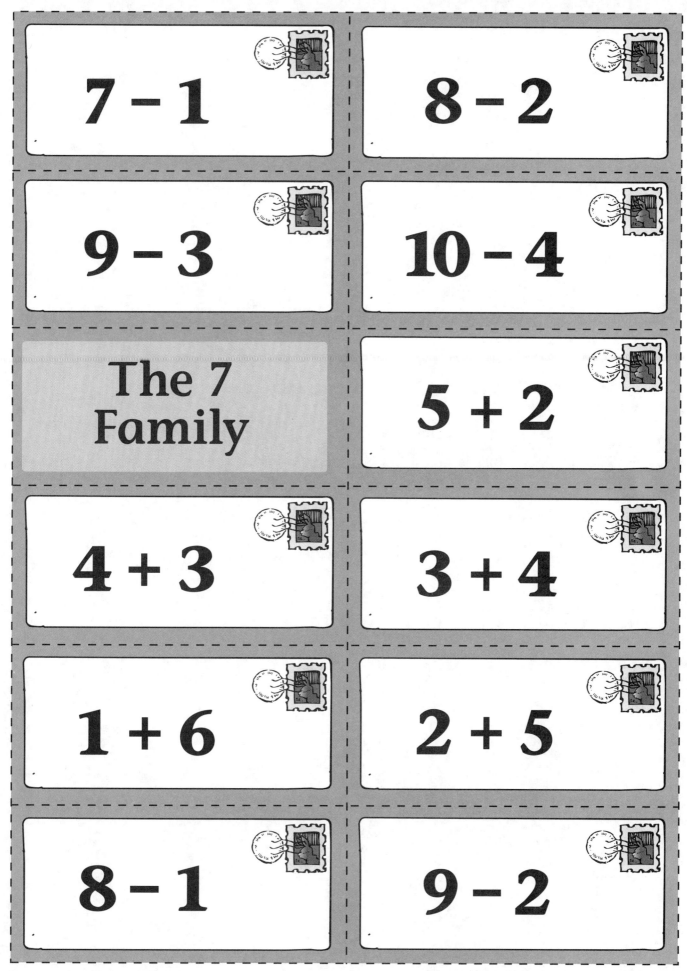

7 − 1

8 − 2

9 − 3

10 − 4

The 7 Family

5 + 2

4 + 3

3 + 4

1 + 6

2 + 5

8 − 1

9 − 2

Math Centers - Take It to Your Seat • EMC 3013

The 8 Family

6 + 2

5 + 3

4 + 4

3 + 5

2 + 6

9 – 1

10 – 2

The 9 Family

7 + 2

6 + 3

4 + 5

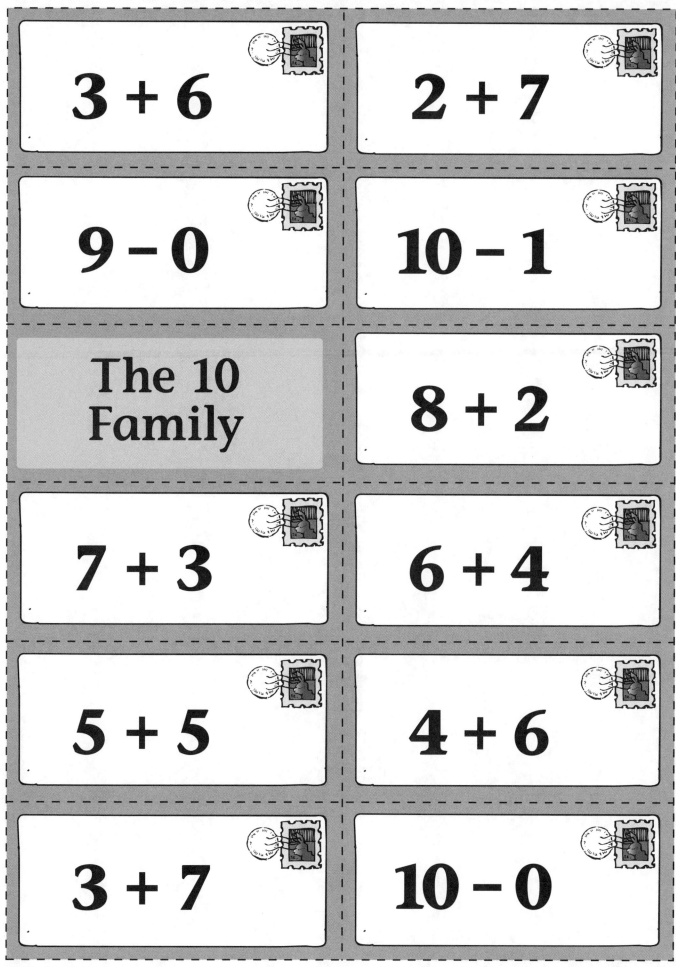

3 + 6

2 + 7

9 − 0

10 − 1

The 10 Family

8 + 2

7 + 3

6 + 4

5 + 5

4 + 6

3 + 7

10 − 0

Telling Time

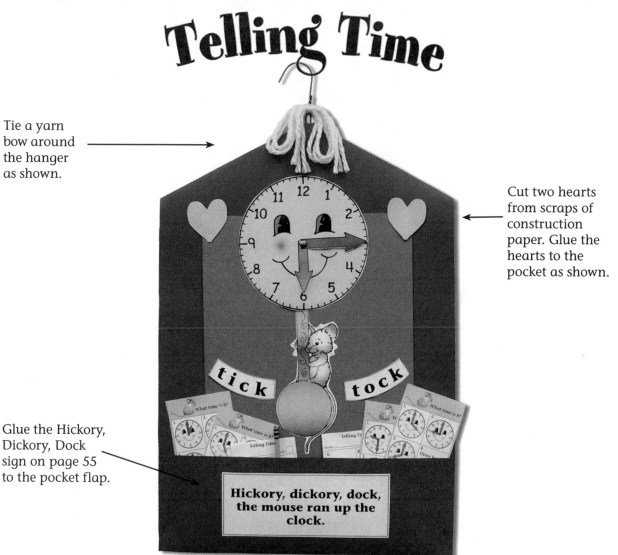

Tie a yarn bow around the hanger as shown.

Cut two hearts from scraps of construction paper. Glue the hearts to the pocket as shown.

Glue the Hickory, Dickory, Dock sign on page 55 to the pocket flap.

tick **tock**

Hickory, dickory, dock, the mouse ran up the clock.

Preparing the Center

1. Using a 17" x 36" (43 x 91 cm) piece of red butcher paper, prepare the top of the basic hanger pocket following the directions on page 3. Glue a 12" x 14" (30.5 x 35.5 cm) sheet of blue construction paper to the center of the pocket. Allow about 1" (2.5 cm) of the paper to slip inside the flap.

2. Laminate and cut out the clock face, hands, pendulum, and pocket sign on pages 53 and 55. Place the top of the pendulum behind the clock and the hands on the front of the clock. Attach them using one large paper fastener.

3. Glue the clock face and the pendulum to the pocket. Then follow the directions above to add details to the hanger pocket.

4. Laminate and cut out the task cards on pages 57, 59, 61, 63, and 65. Place the cards and a supply of the answer forms on page 52 in the clock pocket.

Using the Center

1. The student takes a card out of the clock hanger pocket and reads it.

2. The student writes the answers to questions 1, 2, and 3 on the answer form and then draws hands on the clock face to answer question 4.

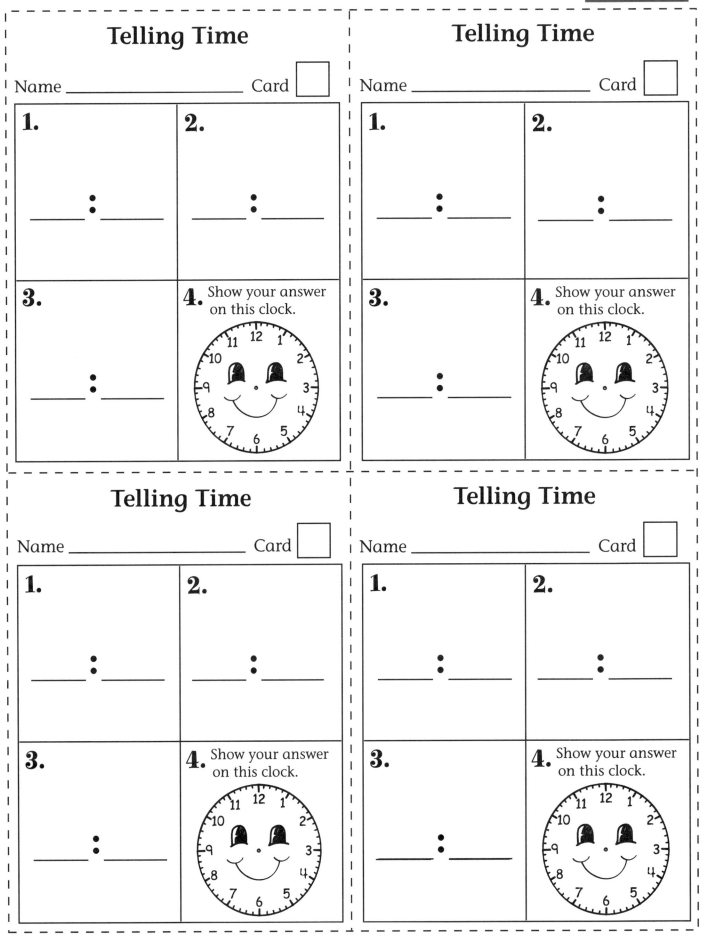

Telling Time

Name _____ Card ☐

1.

___ : ___

2.

___ : ___

3.

___ : ___

4. Show your answer on this clock.

Telling Time

Name _____ Card ☐

1.

___ : ___

2.

___ : ___

3.

___ : ___

4. Show your answer on this clock.

Telling Time

Name _____ Card ☐

1.

___ : ___

2.

___ : ___

3.

___ : ___

4. Show your answer on this clock.

Telling Time

Name _____ Card ☐

1.

___ : ___

2.

___ : ___

3.

___ : ___

4. Show your answer on this clock.

Hickory, dickory, dock, the mouse ran up the clock.

55

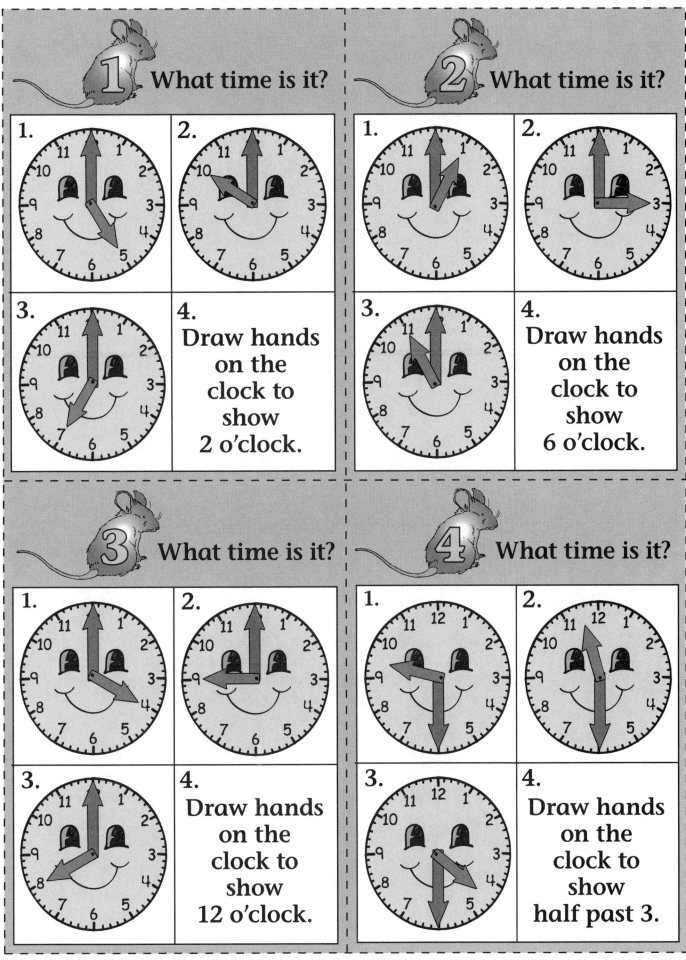

1 **What time is it?**

1.

2.

3.

4.
Draw hands
on the
clock to
show
2 o'clock.

2 **What time is it?**

1.

2.

3.

4.
Draw hands
on the
clock to
show
6 o'clock.

3 **What time is it?**

1.

2.

3.

4.
Draw hands
on the
clock to
show
12 o'clock.

4 **What time is it?**

1.

2.

3.

4.
Draw hands
on the
clock to
show
half past 3.

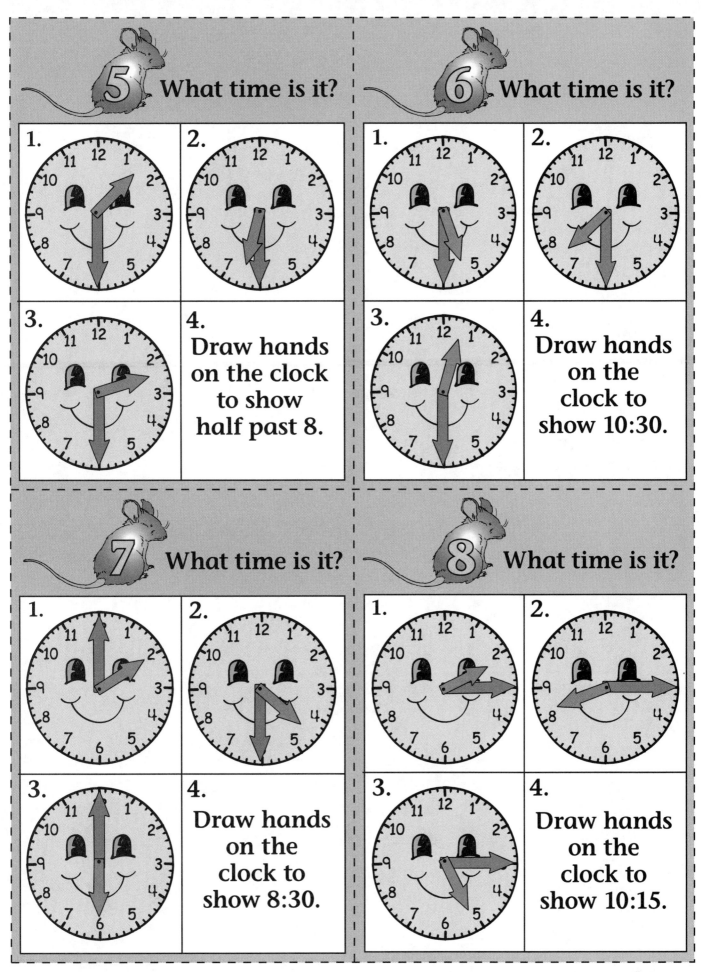

5 What time is it?

1.

2.

3.

4. Draw hands on the clock to show half past 8.

6 What time is it?

1.

2.

3.

4. Draw hands on the clock to show 10:30.

7 What time is it?

1.

2.

3.

4. Draw hands on the clock to show 8:30.

8 What time is it?

1.

2.

3.

4. Draw hands on the clock to show 10:15.

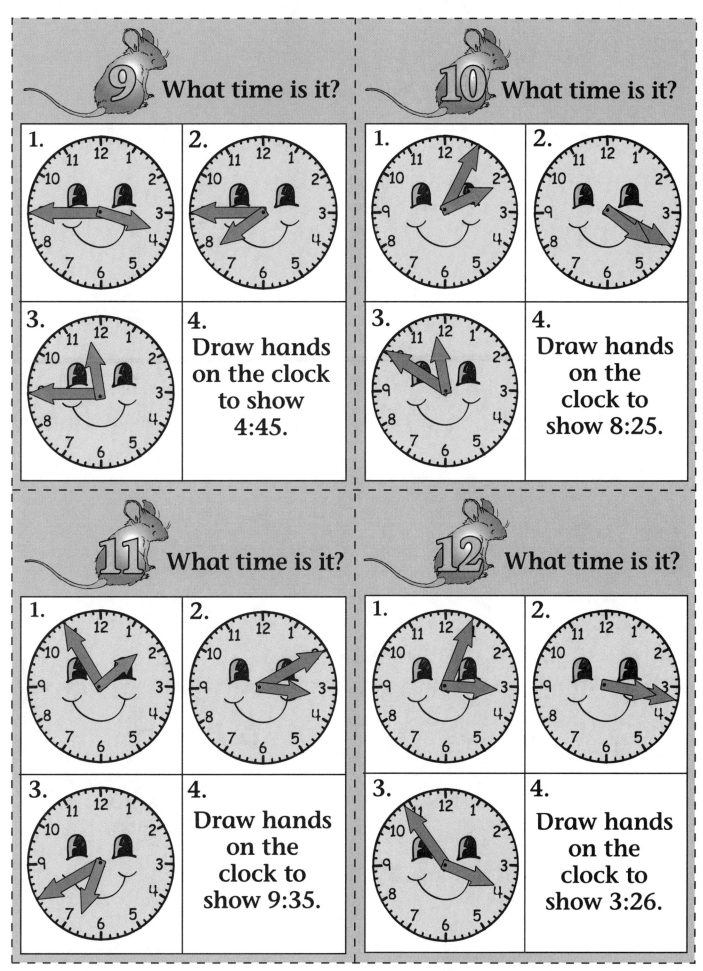

What time is it?

9

1.

2.

3.

4.
Draw hands on the clock to show 4:45.

What time is it?

10

1.

2.

3.

4.
Draw hands on the clock to show 8:25.

What time is it?

11

1.

2.

3.

4.
Draw hands on the clock to show 9:35.

What time is it?

12

1.

2.

3.

4.
Draw hands on the clock to show 3:26.

Math Centers - Take It to Your Seat • EMC 3013

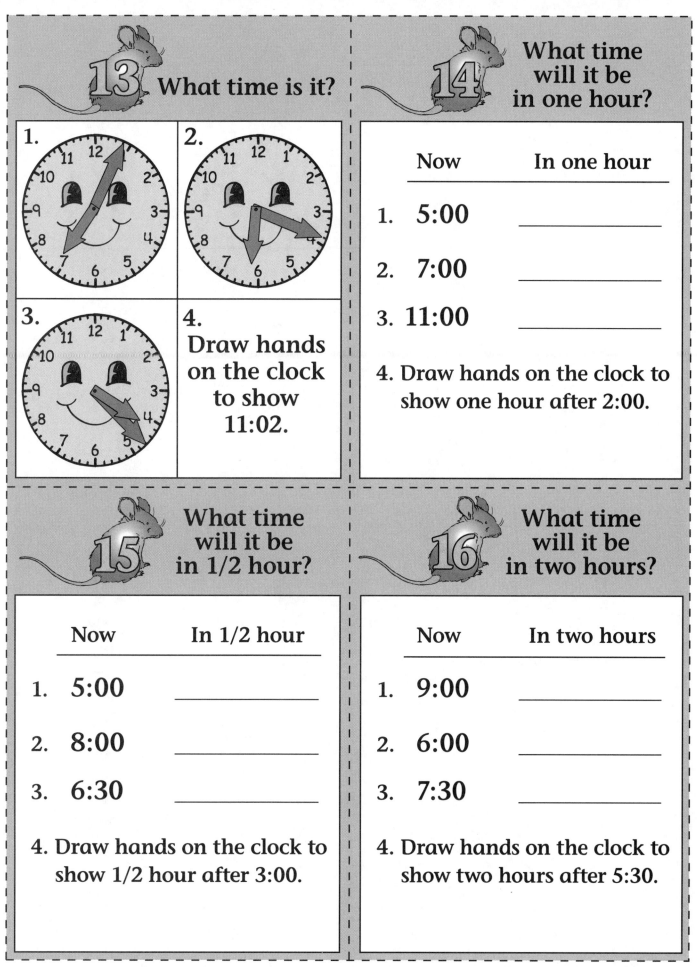

13 What time is it?

1.

2.

3.

4. Draw hands on the clock to show 11:02.

14 What time will it be in one hour?

Now	In one hour
1. **5:00**	_____
2. **7:00**	_____
3. **11:00**	_____

4. Draw hands on the clock to show one hour after 2:00.

15 What time will it be in 1/2 hour?

Now	In 1/2 hour
1. **5:00**	_____
2. **8:00**	_____
3. **6:30**	_____

4. Draw hands on the clock to show 1/2 hour after 3:00.

16 What time will it be in two hours?

Now	In two hours
1. **9:00**	_____
2. **6:00**	_____
3. **7:30**	_____

4. Draw hands on the clock to show two hours after 5:30.

17 What time was it one hour ago?

	Now	One hour ago
1.	**11:00**	_____
2.	**3:00**	_____
3.	**1:30**	_____

4. Draw hands on the clock to show one hour before 7:00.

18 Show your answer on the clock by number 4.

Jill was at the zoo for two hours.

She came at 10:00.

What time did she go home?

19 Show your answer on the clock by number 4.

Ann got to the zoo at 3:00.

She can stay for three hours.

What time must she go home?

20 Show your answer on the clock by number 4.

I left for my friend's house at 10:15.

It took 15 minutes to get to his house.

What time did I get there?

Word Problems

Round the corners of two 5" (13 cm) squares of brown construction paper for the ears. Round the corners of two 3" (7.5 cm) squares of light brown paper. Glue to the inside of the ears.

Round the corners of a 7" (18 cm) square of light brown paper for the snout. Add a nose cut from a 2" (5 cm) square of black paper. Draw in the mouth with a black marking pen.

Round the corners of one side of a 5" x 7" (13 x 18 cm) piece of light brown paper for the tummy. Glue it in place as shown. Write *Word Problems* on the bear's tummy.

Tie a bow of red yarn to the top of the hanger pocket.

Cut eyes from scraps of black and white paper. Glue them in place.

Cut arms from two 5" x 6" (13 x 15 cm) pieces of brown construction paper. Add details with a black marking pen. Glue the straight edge of each arm to the back of the pocket. Wrap the paws around to the front as shown. Tape or glue in place.

Preparing the Center

1. Using a 17" x 36" (43 x 91 cm) piece of brown butcher paper, prepare the top of the basic hanger pocket following the directions on page 3. Using a 6" x 17" (15 x 43 cm) piece of yellow construction paper, add a hat cut to fit the top of the pocket. Add dots or little hearts cut from scraps of colored paper. Then follow the directions above to add details to the hanger pocket.

2. Laminate and cut out the problems on pages 69, 71, 73, 75, and 77. Place them in the bear pocket.

3. Place a supply of the answer forms on page 68 in the pocket.

Using the Center

1. The student takes a word problem out of the bear hanger pocket and reads it.

2. The student then writes the answer to the problem on the answer form. This answer form may be used for multiple cards. Determine in advance where students will keep their answer forms between turns at the center.

Word Problem

Name _____

Card	Answer	Card	Answer
1. _____		**11.** _____	
2. _____		**12.** _____	
3. _____		**13.** _____	
4. _____		**14.** _____	
5. _____		**15.** _____	
6. _____		**16.** _____	
7. _____		**17.** _____	
8. _____		**18.** _____	
9. _____		**19.** _____	
10. _____		**20.** _____	

Word Problems

2.

Big Bear saw 9 bees on the rosebush. 4 more bees came. How many bees are there in all?

Word Problems

4.

Mother Bear took 6 fish from the river. She gave 2 fish to her cub. She ate 3 fish. How many fish were left?

Word Problems

1.

Mother Bear and her three cubs are in a den. How many bears are in the den?

Word Problems

3.

At the zoo I saw…

9 black bears,
3 sun bears, and
6 polar bears.

How many bears did I see in all?

Word Problems

6.

A bear was fishing at the river. Yesterday the bear caught 12 fish. Today the bear caught 7 fish. How many fish did he catch in all?

Word Problems

8.

A bear saw 13 bees on a beehive. 7 bees flew away. How many bees were left?

Word Problems

5.

A bear ate one jar of honey a day. How many jars of honey did the bear eat in one week?

Word Problems

7.

If each bear ate 5 fish, how many fish would 10 bears eat?

Word Problems

9.

If 1 bear has 4 legs, how many legs will 3 bears have?

Word Problems

10.

Belle collects toy bears. She has seven now. How many will she have if she gets three more bears for her birthday?

Word Problems

11.

Mom took us to the zoo to see the new cub. We left home at 2:00. We got to the zoo at 3:00. How long did it take us to get to the zoo?

Word Problems

12.

We got to the zoo at 3:00. We left at 5:00. How long did we stay at the zoo?

Word Problems

13.

There are sixteen books about bears in the library. Sam has read half of them. How many bear books has he read?

Word Problems

14.

23 bears escaped from the zoo. 16 have been caught. How many bears are still loose?

Word Problems

15.

There are three places to see bears at the zoo. If each place has 6 bears, how many bears are there in all?

Word Problems

16.

If one ticket to the zoo costs $4.00, how much will 4 tickets cost?

Word Problems

18.

It costs $3.00 a day to feed a bear in the zoo. How much does it cost to feed a bear for one week?

Word Problems

20.

20 third-graders went to the zoo to study the bears. The teacher needed one parent to walk with each group of five students. How many parents did she need to go on the field trip?

Word Problems

17.

A child's ticket to the zoo costs $4.00. An adult's ticket costs $8.95. How much more does an adult ticket cost than a ticket for a child?

Word Problems

19.

Maggie bought a box of chocolate bear cookies. The box of cookies cost $1.80. She gave the clerk $2.00. How much money did she get back?

Shoebox Centers

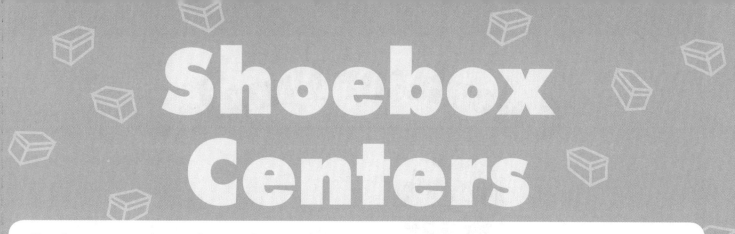

Shoebox centers are easily stored on a table or shelf in the classroom. Students take the centers to their seats to complete a task.

Preparing a Shoebox Center

Materials

- shoebox
- Con-Tact® or butcher paper to fit the box
- copies of patterns provided for each center
- scissors
- craft knife
- double-sided tape
- crayons or marking pens

Steps to Follow

1. Cover the shoebox and lid with Con-Tact® or butcher paper.

2. Laminate and cut out the pattern pieces. Tape them to the shoebox as shown for each center.

3. Laminate and cut out the task cards. Select the cards appropriate for your students and place them in the shoebox.

4. Paper and other materials needed are listed in the directions for each center. Special pencils or erasers for the center themes would be an added motivation.

Calculator Puzzles

Preparing the Center

1. Using the patterns on pages 83 and 85, prepare the robot shoebox following the directions on page 79. Attach the arms with brass paper fasteners.

2. Laminate and cut out the task cards on pages 87, 89, and 91. Place them in the shoebox along with a calculator.

3. Reproduce copies of the answer form on page 81. Place the answer forms, a pencil, and a calculator in the robot box.

Using the Center

1. The student opens the flap, selects a card from the robot shoebox, and then writes its number on the answer form.

2. The student reads the card, uses the calculator to figure out the answer, and then writes the answer on the answer form.

3. Determine in advance how many problems you want the student to do at one time.

 Math Centers - Take It to Your Seat • EMC 3013

Calculator Puzzles

Name _____

Job Card _____

Job Card _____

Job Card _____

Calculator Puzzles

Name _____

Job Card _____

Job Card _____

Job Card _____

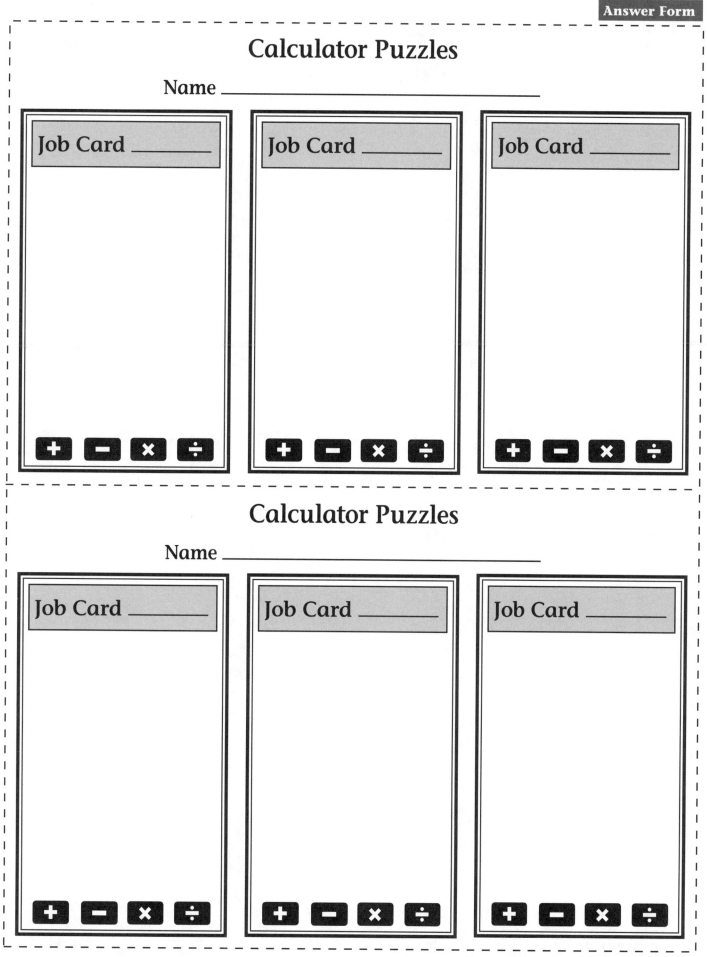

Note: Reproduce these cards to make your own calculator puzzles.

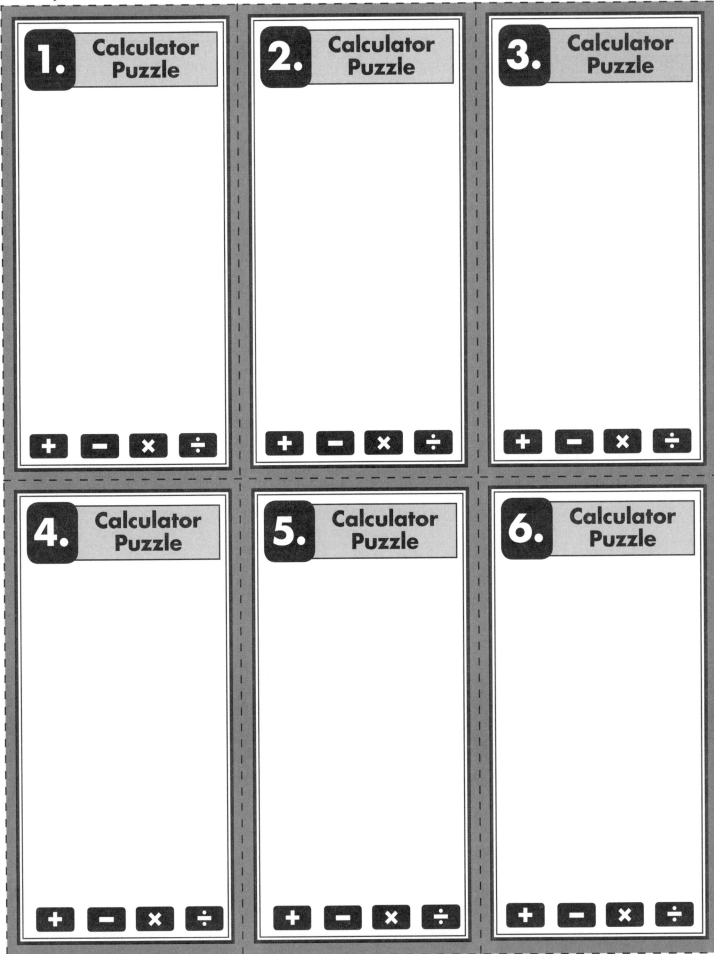

glue

fold

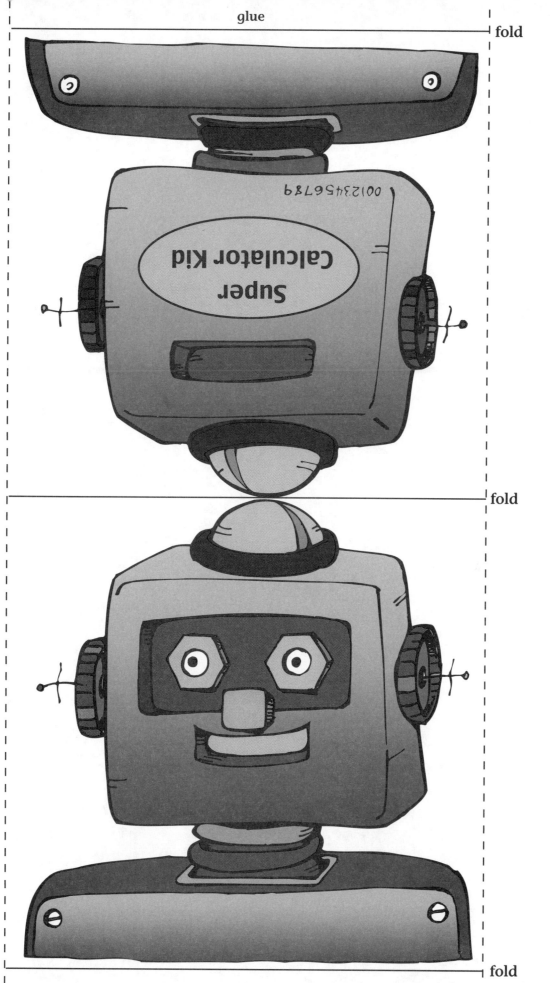

Super Calculator Kid

fold

fold

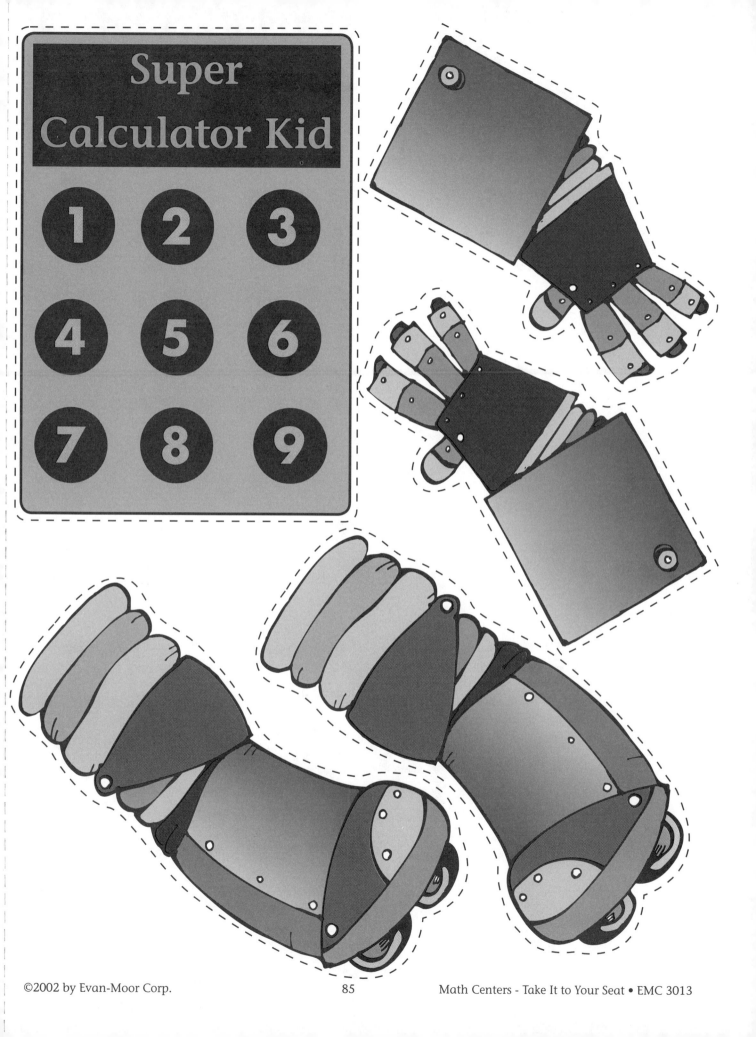

Super
Calculator Kid

1 2 3
4 5 6
7 8 9

 Math Centers - Take It to Your Seat • EMC 3013

1. Calculator Puzzle

Look at your calculator.

1. How many number keys do you see?

2. How many keys have letters?

2. Calculator Puzzle

Draw a picture of your calculator.

Color the keys:

+ ...... blue

– .... green

× ...... red

÷ ...... orange

= ...... purple

3. Calculator Puzzle

Look at your calculator. Write the symbol for:

1. addition

2. subtraction

3. multiplication

4. division

5. equals

4. Calculator Puzzle

Practice using your calculator.

Enter 6

+ 3

– 4

= ?

5. Calculator Puzzle

Practice using your calculator.

Enter 9

– 4

+ 7

= ?

6. Calculator Puzzle

Add these problems using your calculator.

1. $2 + 3 + 1 + 4 =$ _____

2. $10 + 6 - 2 \ =$ _____

3. $9 - 3 - 2 \ =$ _____

4. $10 - 5 + 9 \ =$ _____

7. Calculator Puzzle

Add these problems using your calculator.

1. $7 + 5 + 9 + 6 =$ _____

2. $10 + 18 \ =$ _____

3. $15 + 12 \ =$ _____

4. $69 + 35 \ =$ _____

+ − × ÷

8. Calculator Puzzle

Subtract these problems using your calculator.

1. $9 - 4 - 2 =$ _____

2. $8 - 2 - 3 =$ _____

3. $37 - 15 \ =$ _____

4. $94 - 22 \ =$ _____

+ − × ÷

9. Calculator Puzzle

Add these problems using your calculator.

1. $48 + 57 \ =$ _____

2. $110 + 235 =$ _____

3. $756 + 241 =$ _____

4. $121 + 138 + 116$

$=$ _____

+ − × ÷

10. Calculator Puzzle

Subtract these problems using your calculator.

1. $37 - 19 \ =$ _____

2. $80 - 26 \ =$ _____

3. $497 - 264$

$=$ _____

4. $531 - 236 - 109$

$=$ _____

+ − × ÷

11. Calculator Puzzle

Enter the number of legs on a spider.

Add the number of legs on a horse.

Subtract the number of wings on a bird.

What is your answer?

+ − × ÷

12. Calculator Puzzle

Enter the number of days in a week.

Add the number of eggs in a dozen.

Subtract the number of ears on a monkey.

What is your answer?

+ − × ÷

13. Calculator Puzzle

Enter the number of toes on one foot.

✗ the number of fingers on one hand.

+ the number of wheels on a bicycle.

What is your answer?

| + | − | ✗ | ÷ |

14. Calculator Puzzle

Enter the number of legs on an ant.

✗ the number of arms on an octopus.

− the number of cents in a dime.

What is your answer?

| + | − | ✗ | ÷ |

15. Calculator Puzzle

The factory can build 5 robots a day.

How many robots can be built in 20 days?

| + | − | ✗ | ÷ |

16. Calculator Puzzle

I have three hens. Each hen lays one egg a day.

How many eggs will the three hens lay in one week?

| + | − | ✗ | ÷ |

17. Calculator Puzzle

Which is the largest amount?

$$20 + 19$$
$$17 \times 2$$
$$57 - 28$$
$$99 \div 3$$

| + | − | ✗ | ÷ |

18. Calculator Puzzle

Enter 35009.

Turn your calculator upside down.

Draw a picture of the word you see.

| + | − | ✗ | ÷ |

Patterning

Preparing the Center

1. Using the patterns on pages 95 and 97, prepare the rabbit shoebox following the directions on page 79.

2. Laminate and cut out the patterning pieces on page 99. Put the patterning pieces in a self-closing plastic bag.

3. Laminate and cut out the task cards on pages 101, 103, and 105. Place them in the shoebox.

4. Place a supply of the answer forms on page 94, the bag of patterning pieces, and a pencil in the rabbit box.

Using the Center

1. The student lifts the lid and takes the bag of patterning pieces and a card from the rabbit shoebox.

2. The student reads the card and completes the patterning task using the patterning pieces.

3. The student draws the correct pattern on the answer form.

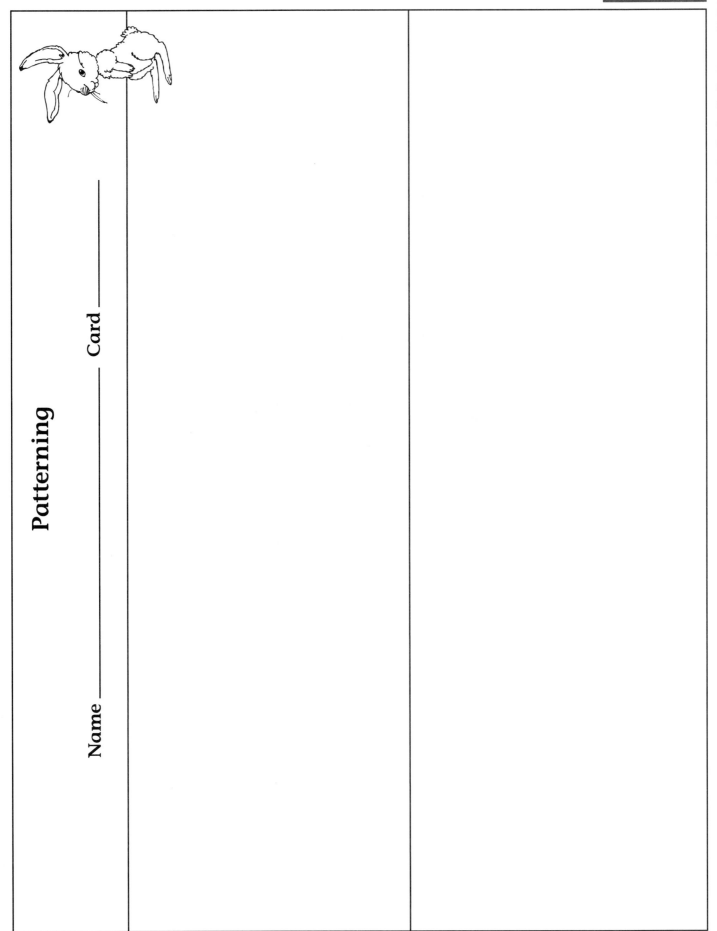

Patterning

Name _____

Card _____

Rabbit Patterns

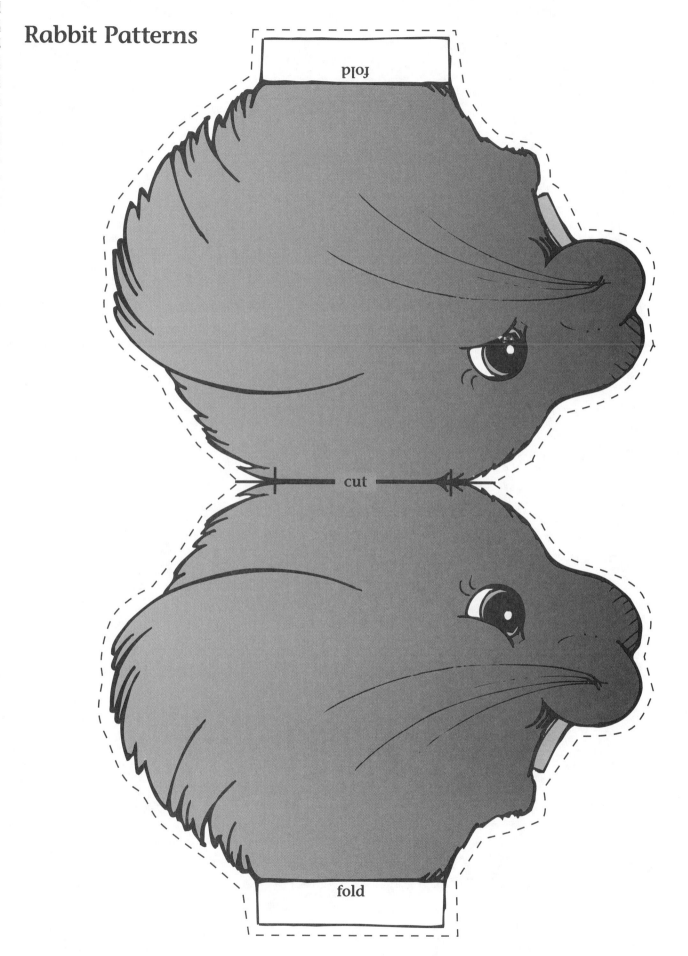

fold

cut

fold

Rabbit Patterns

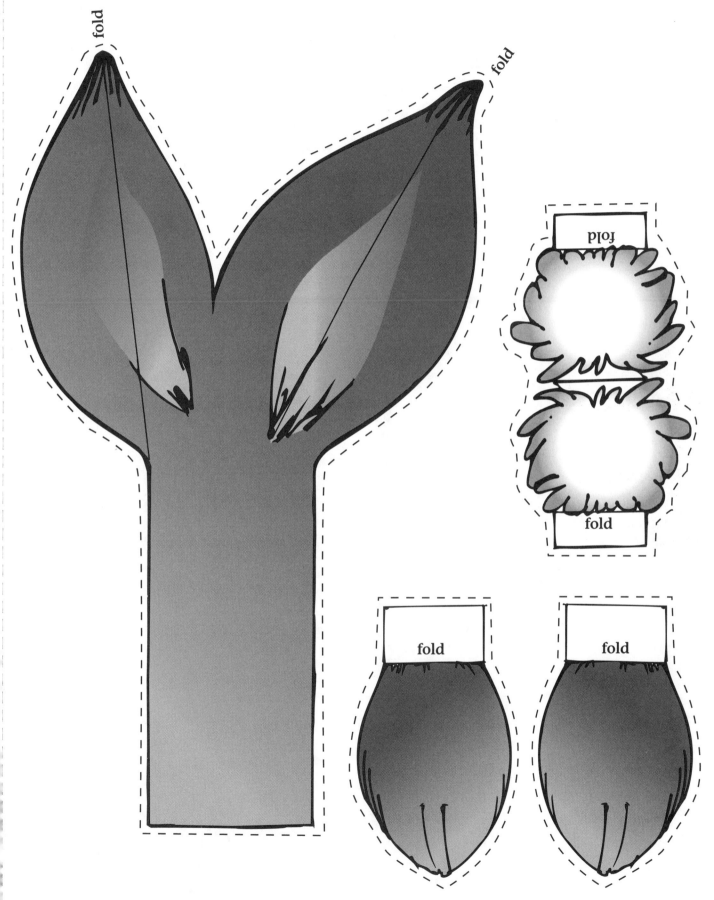

fold

fold

fold

fold

fold

fold

fold

Patterning Pieces

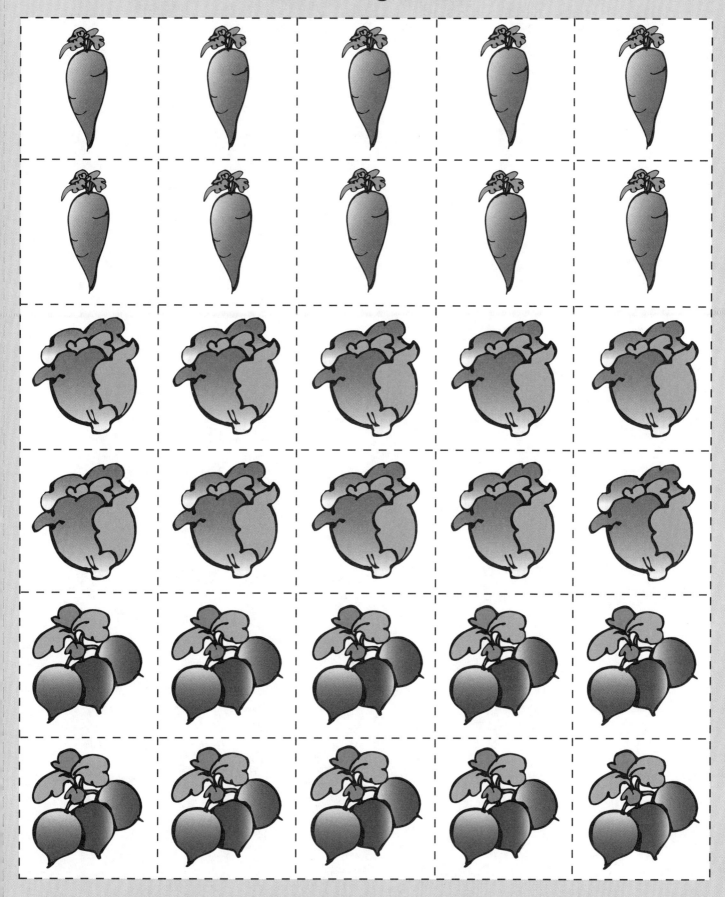

1. What comes next?

Use the vegetables to finish the pattern. Draw the pattern on your answer form.

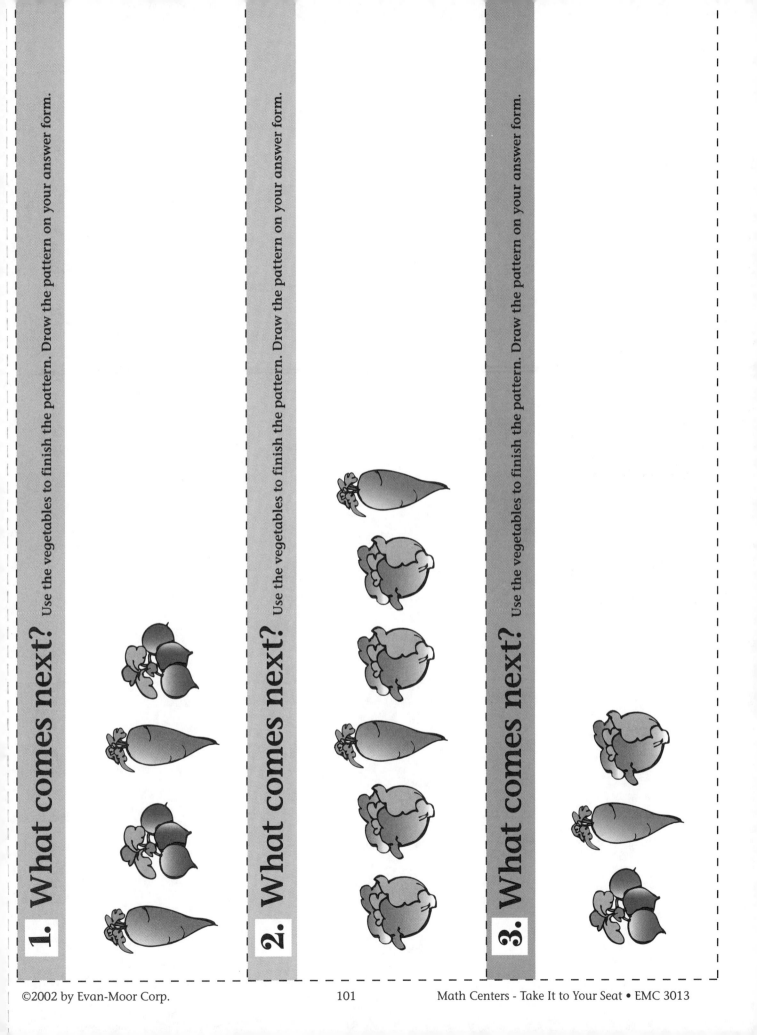

2. What comes next?

Use the vegetables to finish the pattern. Draw the pattern on your answer form.

3. What comes next?

Use the vegetables to finish the pattern. Draw the pattern on your answer form.

4. What comes next?
Use the vegetables to finish the pattern. Draw the pattern on your answer form.

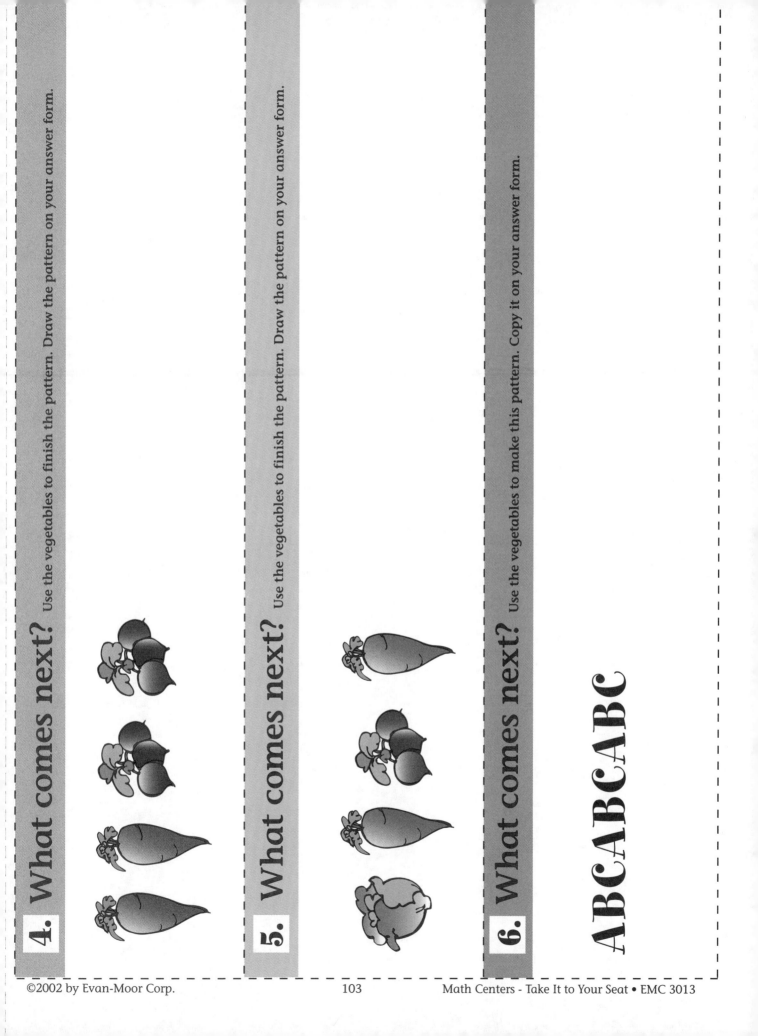

5. What comes next?
Use the vegetables to finish the pattern. Draw the pattern on your answer form.

6. What comes next?
Use the vegetables to make this pattern. Copy it on your answer form.

ABCABCABC

Math Centers - Take It to Your Seat • EMC 3013

7. **What comes next?** Use the vegetables to make this pattern. Copy it on your answer form.

ABBCABBC

8. **What comes next?** Use the vegetables to make this pattern. Copy it on your answer form.

ABCCABCC

9. **What comes next?** Use the vegetables to make a pattern of your own. Copy it on your answer form. Write the name of your pattern.

Linear Measure

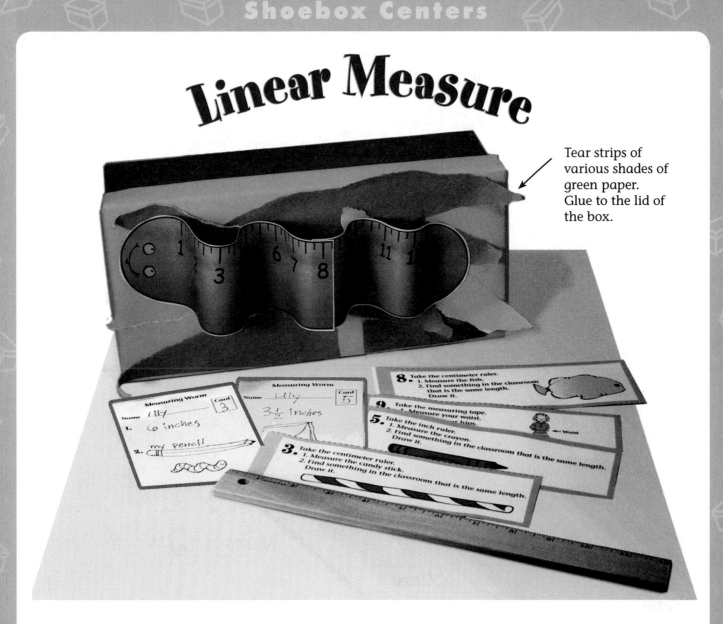

Tear strips of various shades of green paper. Glue to the lid of the box.

Preparing the Center

1. Cut out the patterns on page 109. Glue the measuring worm parts together and laminate. Prepare the measuring worm shoebox following the directions on page 79.

2. Laminate and cut out the task cards on pages 111, 113, and 115. Place them in the shoebox.

3. Place an inch ruler, a centimeter ruler, and a cloth measuring tape in the box.

4. Place a supply of the answer forms on page 108 in the measuring worm shoebox.

Using the Center

1. The student takes a card from the measuring worm shoebox and reads it.

2. Using the correct measuring tool, the student measures to find the answers to the questions on the card.

3. The student writes or draws the answers on the answer form.

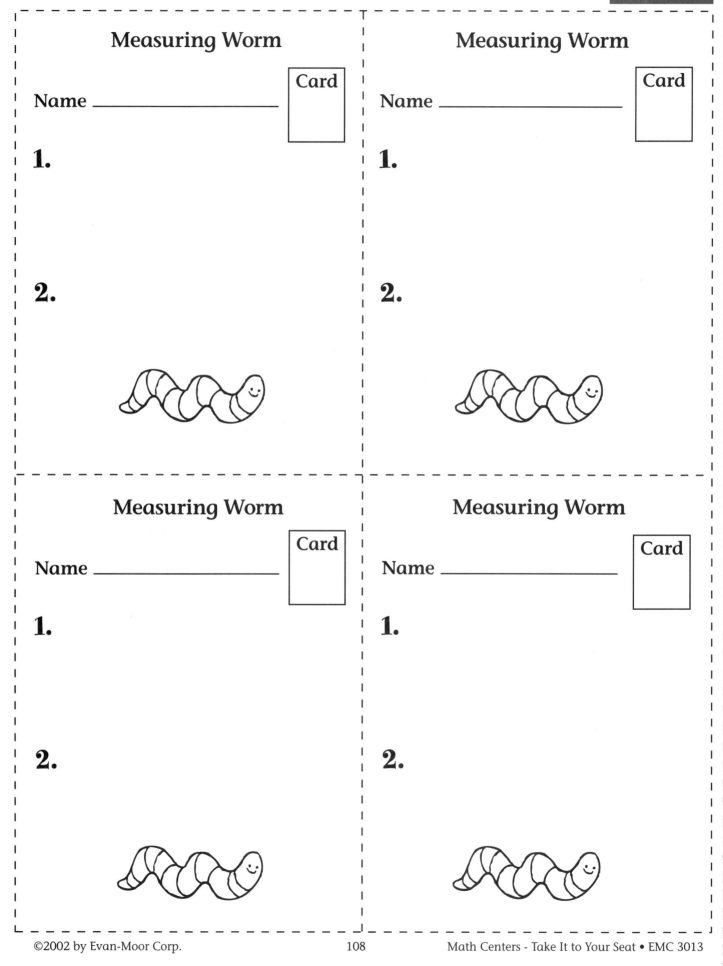

Measuring Worm

Name _____

Card

1.

2.

Measuring Worm

Name _____

Card

1.

2.

Measuring Worm

Name _____

Card

1.

2.

Measuring Worm

Name _____

Card

1.

2.

Math Centers - Take It to Your Seat • EMC 3013

Measuring Worm Patterns

glue

1. Take the inch ruler.
   1. Measure the pencil.
   2. Find something in the classroom that is the same length. Draw it.

2. Take the inch ruler.
   1. Measure the worm.
   2. Find something in the classroom that is the same length. Draw it.

3. Take the centimeter ruler.
   1. Measure the candy stick.
   2. Find something in the classroom that is the same length. Draw it.

4. Take the centimeter ruler.
   1. Measure the pickle.
   2. Find something in the classroom that is the same length. Draw it.

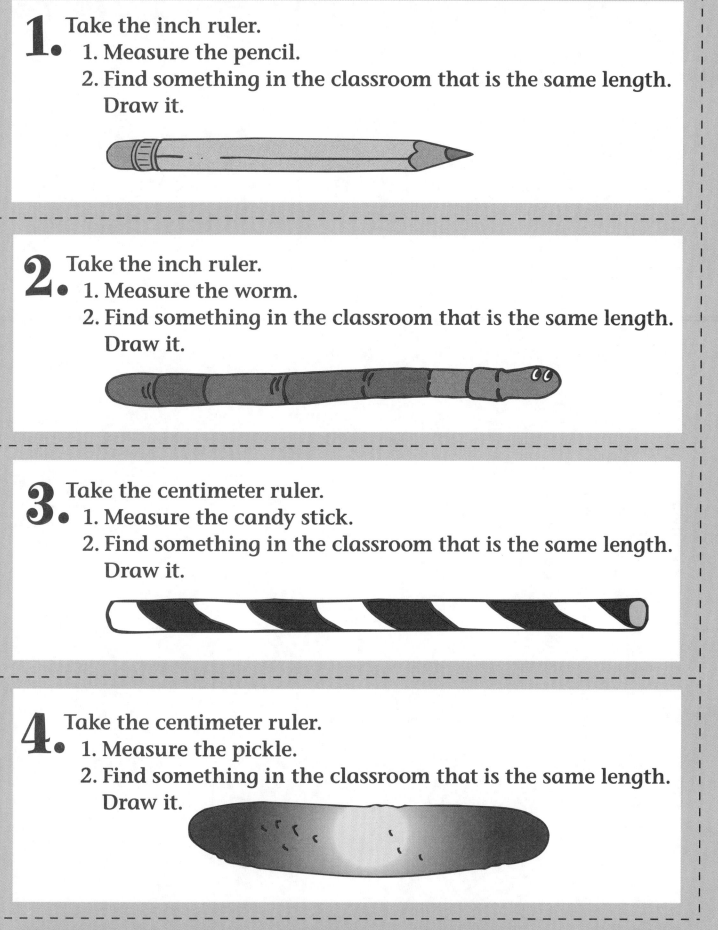

5. Take the inch ruler.
   1. Measure the crayon.
   2. Find something in the classroom that is the same length. Draw it.

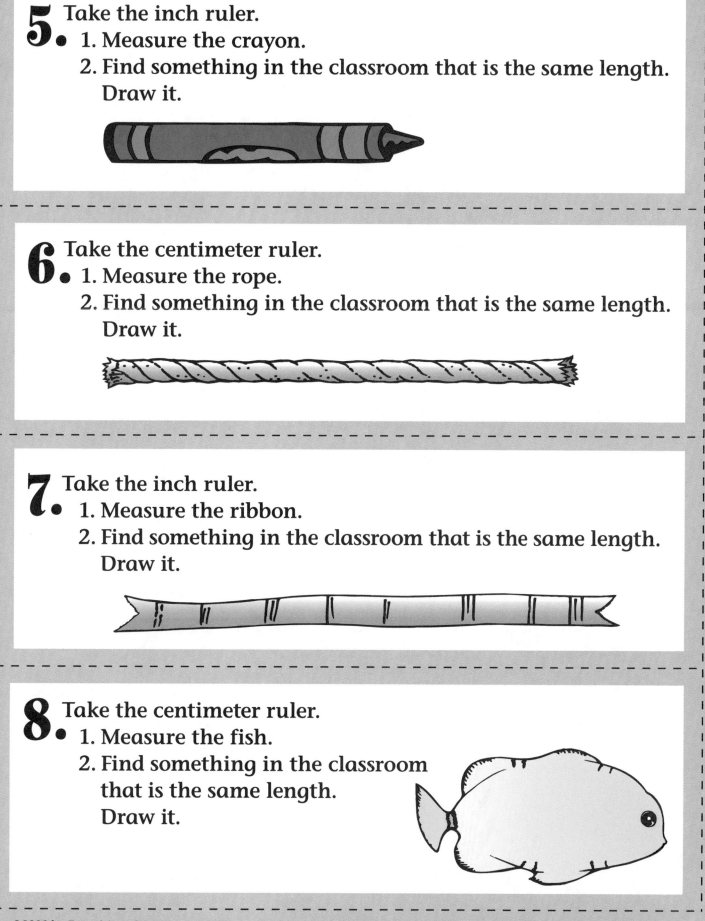

6. Take the centimeter ruler.
   1. Measure the rope.
   2. Find something in the classroom that is the same length. Draw it.

7. Take the inch ruler.
   1. Measure the ribbon.
   2. Find something in the classroom that is the same length. Draw it.

8. Take the centimeter ruler.
   1. Measure the fish.
   2. Find something in the classroom that is the same length. Draw it.

9. Take the measuring tape.
1. Measure your waist.
2. Measure your hips.

Waist

Hips →

10. Take the measuring tape.
1. Measure the length of your desk.
2. Measure the height of your desk.

←Length→

Height

11. Take the measuring tape.
1. With a partner, measure the height of the classroom door.
2. Measure the width of the door.

←Width→

Height

12. Take the measuring tape.
1. With a partner, measure to find out how tall you are.
2. Find someone in the room who is the same height. Write the person's name on the answer form.

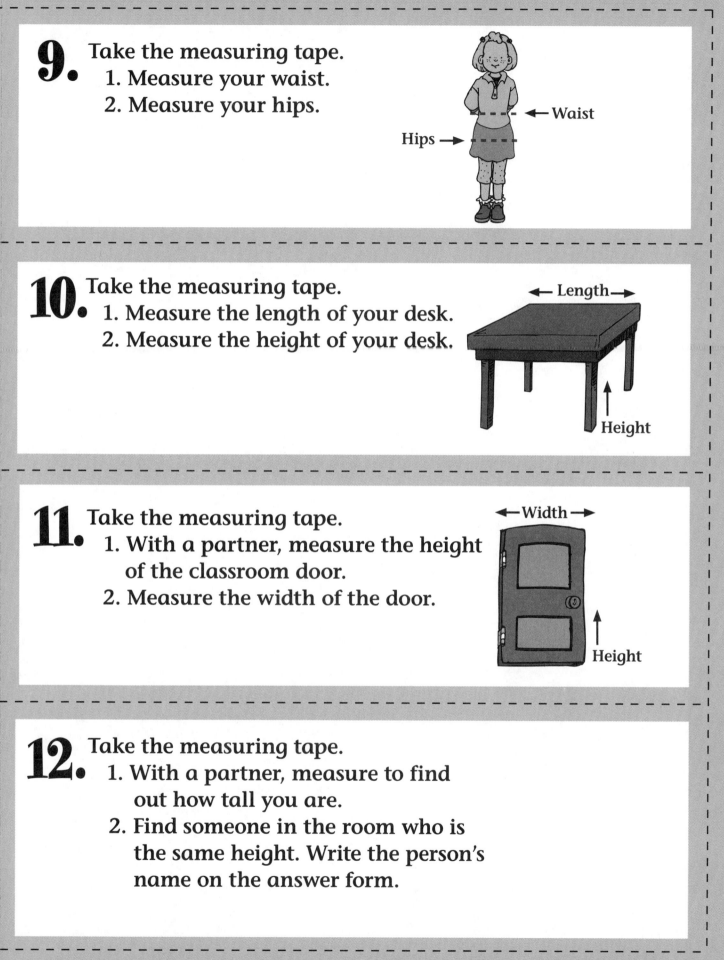

Number Names

Preparing the Center

1. Using the patterns on pages 119 and 121, prepare the sea otter shoebox following the directions on page 79.

2. Laminate and cut out the number cards on page 123 and the task cards on pages 125, 127, 129, 131, 133, and 135. Sort the cards by color. Place all cards of the same color in a separate envelope. Laminate and cut out the labels on page 121. Glue the labels to the appropriate envelopes.

   Set 1—green cards for matching number words and sets of pictures

   Set 2—red cards for addition and subtraction using number words

   Set 3—yellow cards for reading number words above twenty

3. Reproduce copies of the answer form on page 118. Place a supply of answer forms, the envelopes of cards, and a pencil in the sea otter box.

Using the Center

1. The student takes an envelope of cards from the otter box.

2. The student reads a card, completes the task, and writes the answer on the answer form.

Number Names

Name _____   Set: green   red   yellow

1. _____   7. _____

2. _____   8. _____

3. _____   9. _____

4. _____   10. _____

5. _____   11. _____

6. _____   12. _____

Number Names

Name _____   Set: green   red   yellow

1. _____   7. _____

2. _____   8. _____

3. _____   9. _____

4. _____   10. _____

5. _____   11. _____

6. _____   12. _____

Math Centers - Take It to Your Seat • EMC 3013

Otter Pattern

Number
Names

Kelp Patterns and Envelope Labels

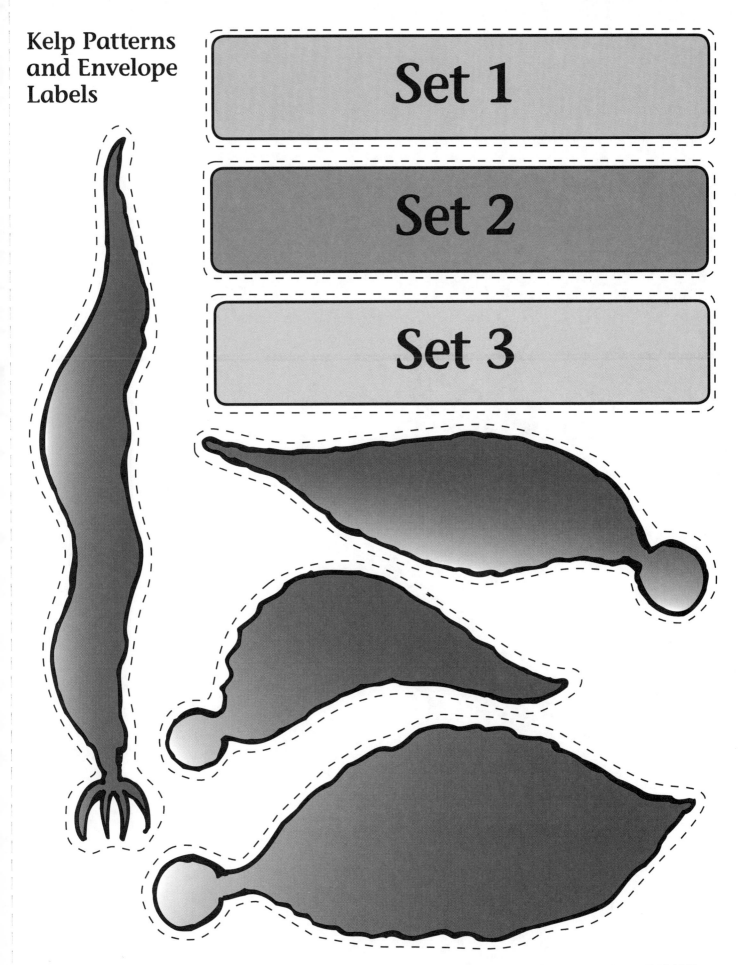

Set 1

Set 2

Set 3

Number Cards

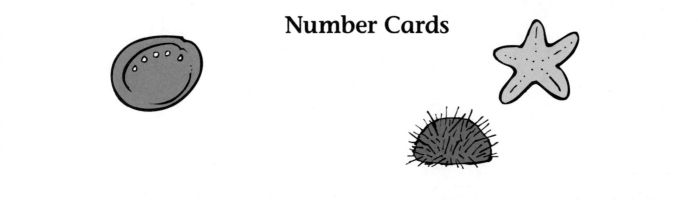

one	two	three
four	five	six
seven	eight	nine
ten	eleven	twelve

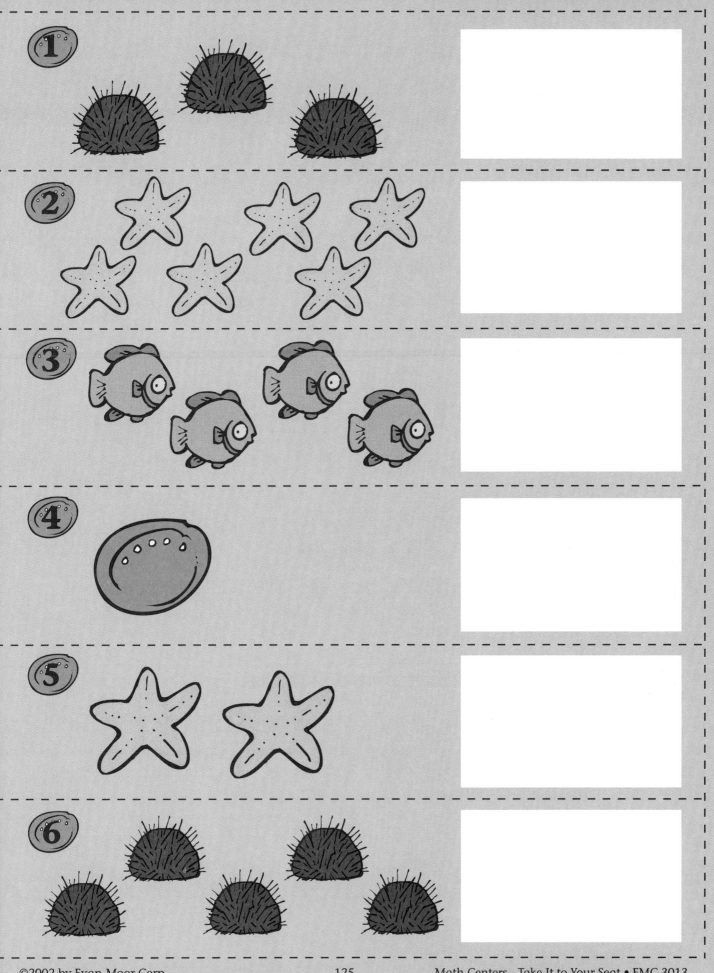

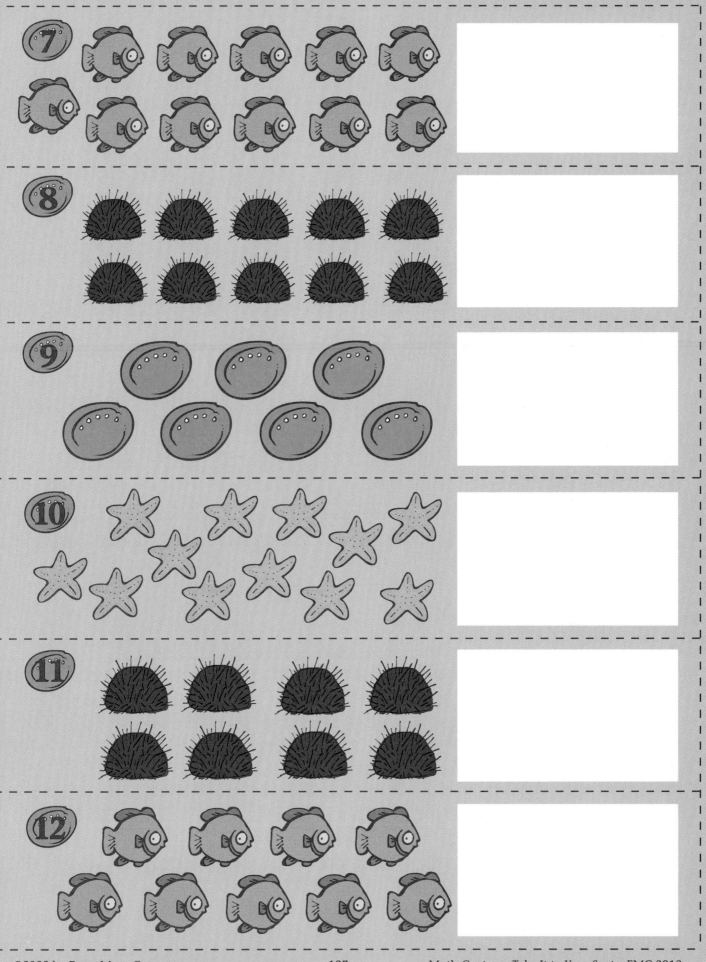

1

two + six =

2

four + three + two =

3

seven – six =

4

five + one =

5

ten – four =

6

eight – three =

 Math Centers - Take It to Your Seat • EMC 3013

7

twelve − ten =

 8

six + six =

 9

two + four + six =

 10

ten − seven + three =

 11

eleven − eight + one =

 12

four + seven =

1 twenty-eight

2 fifty-nine

3 seventy-four

4 thirty-seven

5 eighty-two

6 ninety-nine

7

eight hundred

 8

one hundred seventy-one

 9

five hundred sixty-six

10

seven hundred forty-eight

11

three hundred fifteen

12

four hundred eighty-three

Folder Centers

Folder centers are easily stored in a box or file crate in the classroom. Students take a folder to their seats to complete the task.

Preparing Folder Centers

Materials

- folders with pockets
- marking pens
- glue
- cellophane tape

Steps to Follow

1. Laminate and cut out the cover picture. Glue it to the front of the folder.
2. Tape the edge of the pockets closed as shown.
3. Place answer forms, writing paper, and any other supplies in the left-hand pocket.
4. Place task cards or envelopes in the right-hand pocket.

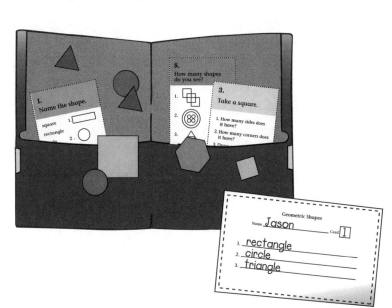

Geometric Shapes

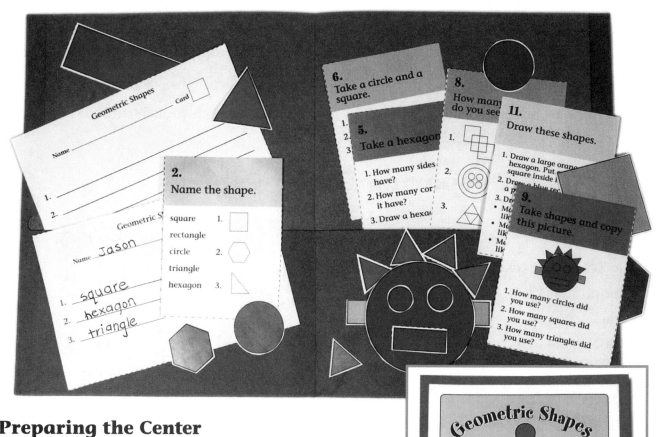

Preparing the Center

1. Prepare a folder following the directions on page 137. Laminate and cut out the cover picture on page 141. Attach it to the front of the folder.

2. Laminate and cut out the geometric shapes on page 143. (Page 140 is reproducible if you need additional shapes.) Place these in a self-closing plastic bag or a large envelope. Place them in the left-hand side of the pocket.

3. Laminate and cut out the task cards on pages 145, 147, and 149. Place them in the right-hand pocket of the folder.

4. Reproduce a supply of the answer forms on page 139. Place them in the left-hand pocket of the folder.

Using the Center

1. The student selects a card and reads the task.

2. Then the student solves the problem, using the geometric shapes when appropriate.

3. The student writes or draws the answer on the answer form.

     Math Centers - Take It to Your Seat • EMC 3013

Geometric Shapes

Name _____ Card ☐

1. _____

2. _____

3. _____

Geometric Shapes

Name _____ Card ☐

1. _____

2. _____

3. _____

Note: Reproduce this page for additional geometric shapes.

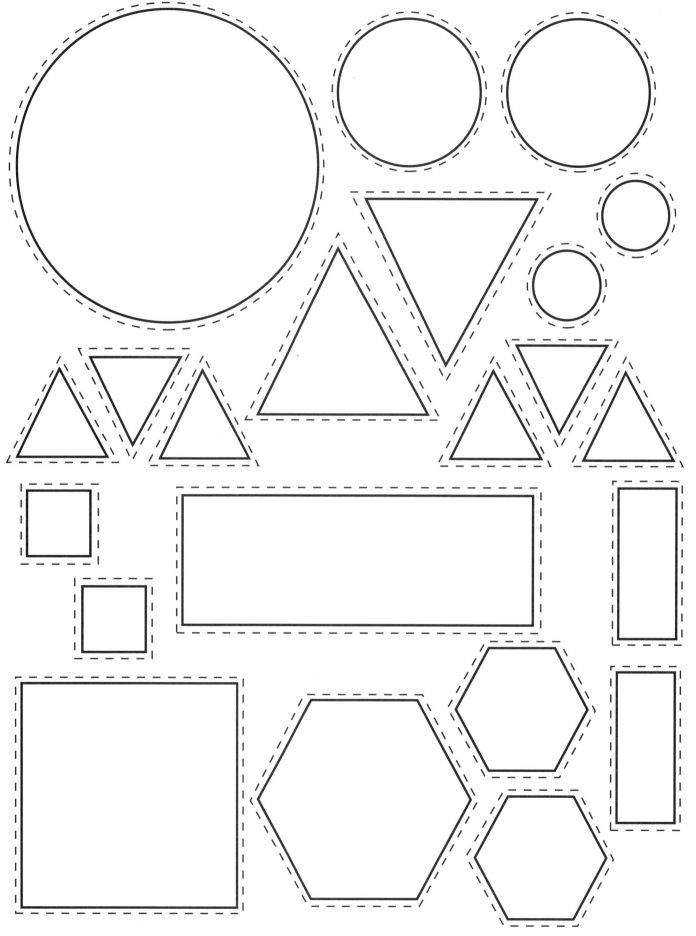

Math Centers - Take It to Your Seat • EMC 3013

Geometric Shapes

Math Centers - Take It to Your Seat • EMC 3013

1.

Name the shape.

square   1.

rectangle

circle   2.

triangle

hexagon   3.

2.

Name the shape.

square   1.

rectangle

circle   2.

triangle

hexagon   3.

3.

Take a square.

1. How many sides does it have?

2. How many corners does it have?

3. Draw a square.

4.

Take a triangle.

1. How many sides does it have?

2. How many corners does it have?

3. Draw a triangle.

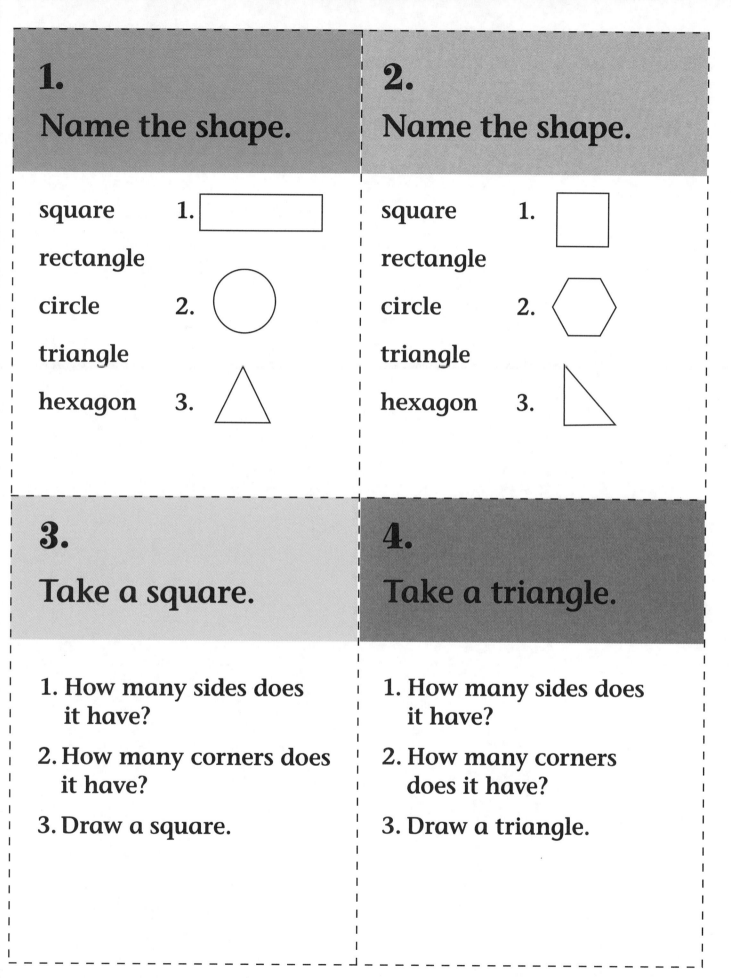

5.
Take a hexagon.

1. How many sides does it have?

2. How many corners does it have?

3. Draw a hexagon.

6.
Take a circle and a square.

1. How are they the same?

2. How are they different?

3. Draw a circle inside a square.

7.
Take a square, a triangle, and a rectangle.

1. How are they the same?

2. How are they different?

3. Draw a square. Make a rectangle under the square. Make a triangle above the square.

8.
How many shapes do you see?

1.

2.

3.

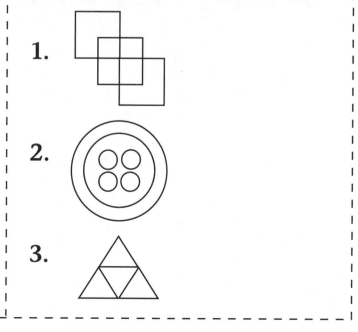

9.
Take shapes and copy this picture.

1. How many circles did you use?
2. How many squares did you use?
3. How many triangles did you use?

10.
Take shapes and copy this picture.

1. How many triangles did you use?
2. How many hexagons did you use?
3. How many circles did you use?

11.
Draw these shapes.

1. Draw a large orange hexagon. Put a small red square inside it.
2. Draw a blue rectangle. Put a purple triangle on top of it.
3. Draw three circles in a row.
   • Make the first circle look like a button.
   • Make the second circle look like a balloon.
   • Make the last circle look like a cookie.

12.
Take some shapes. Make a picture.

Copy the picture on your answer form.

Math Challenges

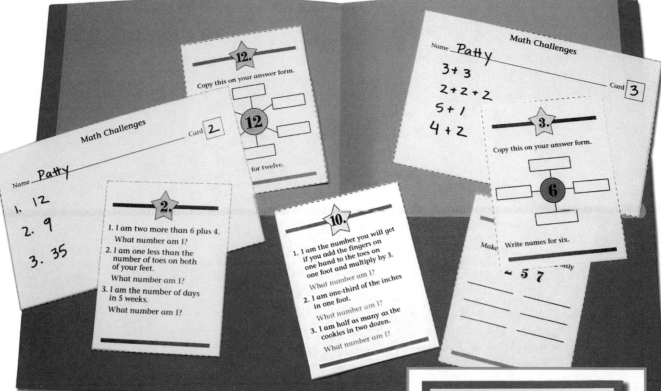

Preparing the Center

1. Prepare a folder following the directions on page 137. Laminate and cut out the cover picture on page 153. Attach it to the front of the folder.

2. Laminate and cut out the task cards on pages 155, 157, and 159. Place them in the right-hand pocket of the folder.

3. Reproduce a supply of the answer forms on page 152. Place them in the left-hand pocket of the folder.

Using the Center

1. The student selects and reads a card.

2. Then the student writes the answer on the answer form. Some cards require students to copy material onto the answer form before answering the problem.

Math Challenges

Name _____ Card [ ]

Math Challenges

Name _____ Card [ ]

Math Challenges

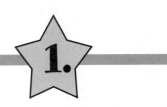

1.

1. Add me to myself and you will have the number 8.

   What number am I?

2. I am the number of eggs in a dozen.

   What number am I?

3. I am the number of sides of a triangle plus the number of sides of a square.

   What number am I?

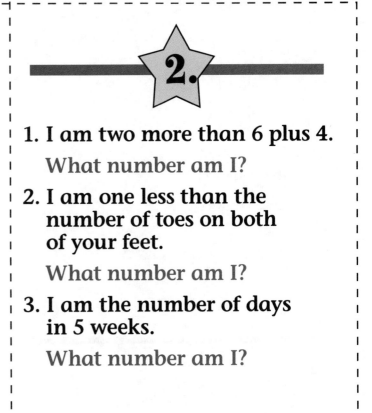

2.

1. I am two more than 6 plus 4.

   What number am I?

2. I am one less than the number of toes on both of your feet.

   What number am I?

3. I am the number of days in 5 weeks.

   What number am I?

3.

Copy this on your answer form.

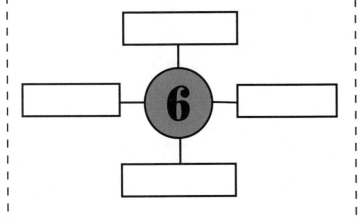

Write names for six.

4.

Copy this on your answer form.

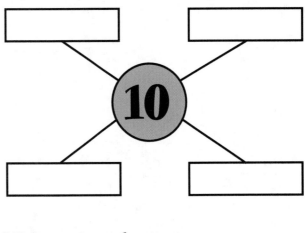

Write names for ten.

5.

Make six numbers using only

2   5   7

_____   _____

_____   _____

_____   _____

6.

Make six numbers using only

9   4   6

_____   _____

_____   _____

_____   _____

7.

1. I am two more than 2 × 5.
   What number am I?

2. I am three less than 10 – 2.
   What number am I?

3. I am the number of legs
   on an ant plus the number of
   arms on an octopus.

   What number am I?

8.

Copy this on your answer form.
Make the numbers add up to 12
in all directions. Use each
number only once.

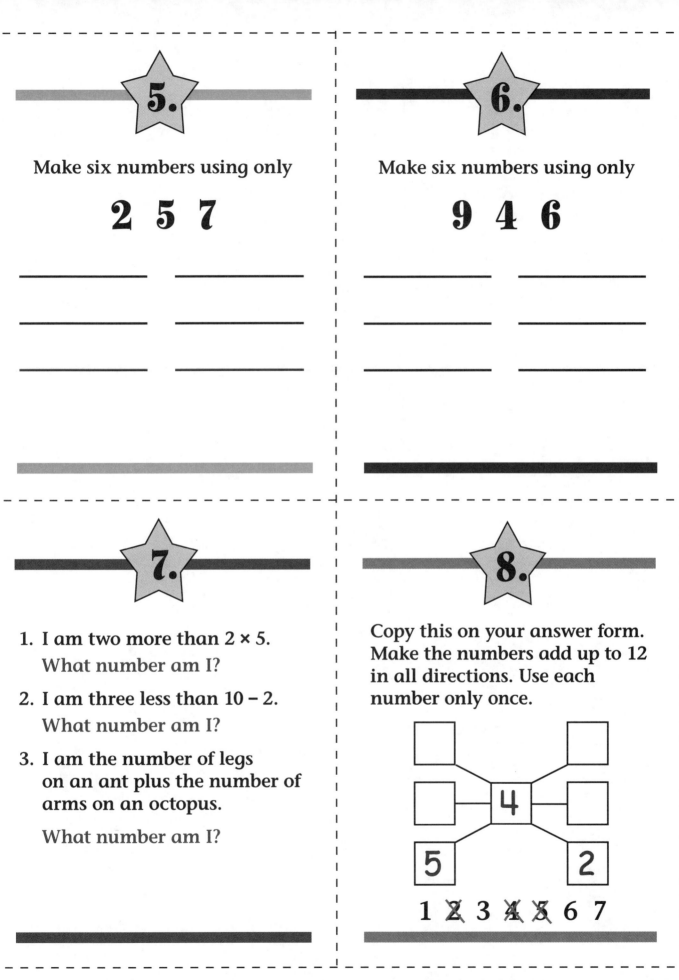

1 2̶ 3 4̶ 5̶ 6 7

1. I am one-half of a dozen.

   What number am I?

2. I am twice as many as the legs on a horse.

   What number am I?

3. I am three times as many as the wheels on a wagon minus the wheels on a bike.

   What number am I?

1. I am the number you will get if you add the fingers on one hand to the toes on one foot and multiply by 3.

   What number am I?

2. I am one-third of the inches in one foot.

   What number am I?

3. I am half as many as the cookies in two dozen.

   What number am I?

1. I am the number you will get if you subtract the days in one week from the eggs in one dozen.

   What number am I?

2. I am twice as many as 3 × 3.

   What number am I?

3. I am five times the number of legs on a dog.

   What number am I?

Copy this on your answer form.

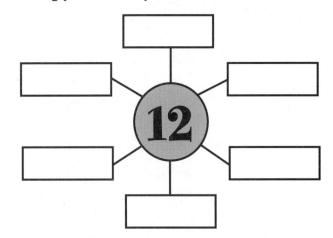

Write names for twelve.

Ordinal Numbers

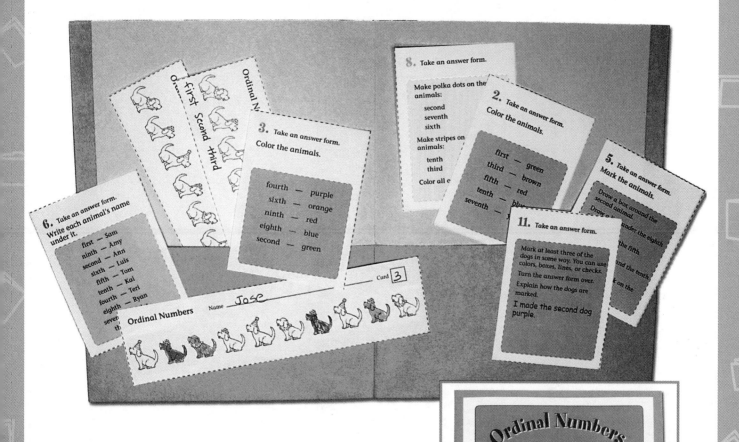

Preparing the Center

1. Prepare a folder following the directions on page 137. Laminate and cut out the cover picture on page 185. Attach it to the front of the folder.

2. Laminate and cut out the task cards on pages 187, 189, and 191. Place them in the right-hand pocket of the folder.

3. Reproduce a supply of the answer forms on page 184. Place them in the left-hand pocket of the folder.

Using the Center

1. The student selects and reads a task card.

2. Then the student writes or draws the answer on the answer form.

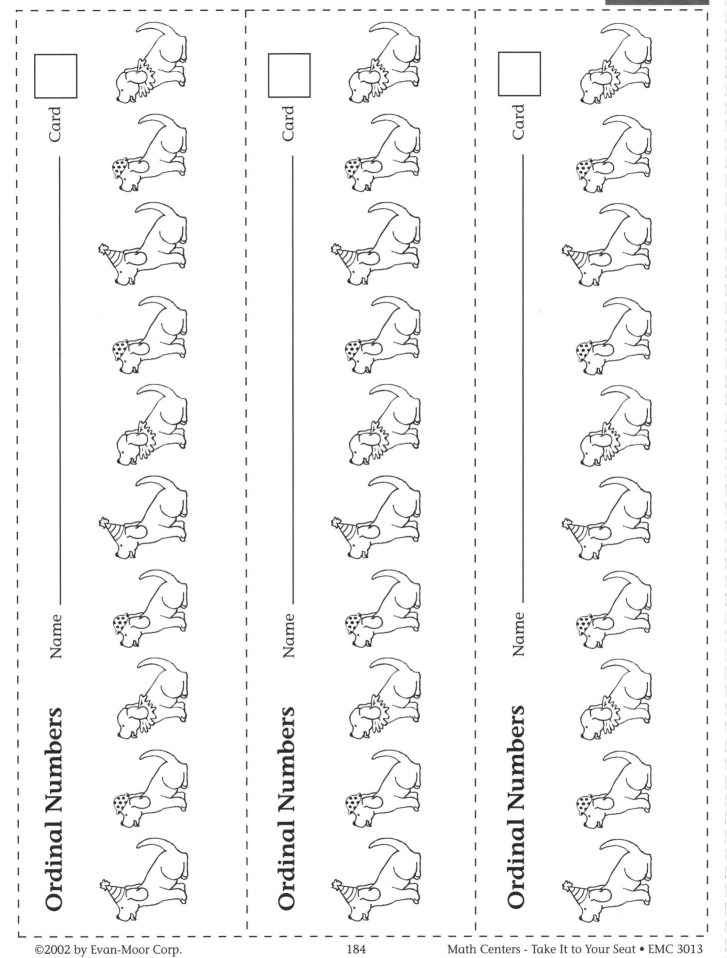

Ordinal Numbers

Name _____

Card [ ]

Ordinal Numbers

Name _____

Card [ ]

Ordinal Numbers

Name _____

Card [ ]

Ordinal Numbers

1. Take an answer form.

Write these numbers in order under the pictures.

first   third   fifth

tenth   second   seventh

fourth   eighth   sixth

ninth

2. Take an answer form.

Color the animals.

first   —   green

third   —   brown

fifth   —   red

tenth   —   blue

seventh   —   yellow

3. Take an answer form.

Color the animals.

fourth   —   purple

sixth   —   orange

ninth   —   red

eighth   —   blue

second   —   green

4. Take an answer form.

Mark the animals.

Make an **X** on the first animal.

Draw a line under the sixth animal.

Draw a ring around the ninth animal.

Draw a box around the fourth animal.

Make a check mark on the third animal.

5. Take an answer form.

Mark the animals.

Draw a box around the second animal.

Draw a line under the eighth animal.

Make an **X** on the fifth animal.

Draw a ring around the tenth animal.

Make a check mark on the ninth animal.

6. Take an answer form.

Write each animal's name under it.

first — Sam

ninth — Amy

second — Ann

sixth — Luis

fifth — Tom

tenth — Kai

fourth — Teri

eighth — Ryan

seventh — Kim

third — Sue

7. Take an answer form.

Write your name under the last animal.

Write how old you are under the first animal.

Write your teacher's name under the fifth animal.

Write the number of your classroom under the eighth animal.

Color the third animal your favorite color.

8. Take an answer form.

Make polka dots on these animals:

second

seventh

sixth

Make stripes on these animals:

tenth

third

Color all of the other animals.

9. Take an answer form.

Draw a ball balanced on the nose of each of these dogs:

sixth   second

third   tenth

eighth   fifth

10. Take an answer form.

Draw a box around the dog **after** the sixth dog.

Draw a line under the dog **before** the third dog.

Color the first and the last dogs.

11. Take an answer form.

Mark at least three of the dogs in some way. You can use colors, boxes, lines, or checks.

Turn the answer form over.

Explain how the dogs are marked.

I made the second dog purple.

12. Take an answer form.

Turn it over and draw these animals in order.

first — elephant

second — bear

third — duck

fourth — lion

fifth — monkey